FIVE DEANS

*

SIDNEY DARK

*

FIVE DEANS

John Colet
John Donne
Jonathan Swift
Arthur Penrhyn Stanley
William Ralph Inge

*

KENNIKAT PRESS/PORT WASHINGTON, N. Y.

FIVE DEANS

First published 1928
Reissued in 1969 by Kennikat Press
Library of Congress Catalog Card No: 70-86011
SBN 8046-0555-6

Manufactured by Taylor Publishing Company   Dallas, Texas

ESSAY AND GENERAL LITERATURE INDEX REPRINT SERIES

CONTENTS

5

I N the studies in this book, I have been mainly concerned
to suggest the relation of each of the individuals whom
I have considered to the movements and reactions of his
time. Of the five Deans, Donne and Swift were far more
distinguished as men of letters than as Churchmen, and
Dr. Inge is far more interested in philosophy than in piety.
But it is mainly as Churchmen that I have considered the
three Deans of St. Paul's, the one Dean of Westminster
and the one Dean of St. Patrick's, as Churchmen and as
typical representatives of the English Church in the years
immediately before the Reformation, in the years that
immediately followed it, in the eighteenth, in the nineteenth and in the twentieth centuries. It may be suggested, not unjustly, that there is no place for Swift in a
volume devoted to ecclesiastics and ecclesiastical affairs.
Thackeray would have it that the great ironist was a great
scoundrel, but no man has suggested that he was a great
Churchman. To me the fact of importance is that Swift
was a Churchman at all. The Church was to him and to
Donne the only possible means of livelihood. That they
were ordained is much less a reflection on their characters
than a criticism of the Church and a demonstration of its
character in the times in which they lived.

Action and reaction have marked the history of the
English Church during the last five centuries as they mark
the history of every institution in all the ages. The high
hopes of the Oxford humanists at the beginning of the
sixteenth century were swamped in the chaos of the
Reformation with its destruction of European unity and
its sorry gift to the world of a new, colourless, negative
religion. The fight of the English Church to preserve
something of its Catholic character against the eager

onslaughts of the Puritans lasted from Elizabeth to the Non-jurors who, though they went out into a lonely and arid wilderness, were responsible for the religious revival of the last two decades of the seventeenth century which left as a legacy to the Church two great societies – the Society for the Propagation of the Gospel and the Society for Promoting Christian Knowledge. There followed the dead years of the eighteenth century with their prevailing Latitudinarianism and the decay of the Church to a spiritual deadness against which Methodism and the Evangelical revival were the revolt. Methodism, almost against the will of Wesley, grew into a schism, and the evangelical revival had no great lasting effect on the life of the Church itself, which, in the years immediately before the beginning of the Oxford Movement, was as worldly and as dead as it had been in the preceding century.

From 1833 until to-day two antagonistic influences have contended for supremacy within the English Church. I have endeavoured to make the character of these influences clear in my study of Dean Stanley who, while himself a Liberal Erastian, had a toleration which was all his own and which was shared neither by his master, Arnold, nor by the Liberal Erastians of our time who still secure the most desirable preferment and sit in the seats of the ecclesiastical mighty. Stanley was the apostle, if he was not the inventor, of comprehensiveness. Arnold would have driven the Tractarians out of the Church into which he was eager to welcome Unitarians. Stanley defended Pusey as he defended Colenso. He was perfectly consistent, because if the Church of England is, as he contended, mainly to be regarded as an invaluable national possession, then it is clear that the wider its boundaries, the better.

On the other hand, the assertion that the Church of England is the Church Catholic in England, the heir of the ages, bound by the generally accepted creeds and traditions, is a flat contradiction of the national church theory which implies the creation by God's providence of a Church particularly suited for God's Englishmen.

It is true that men holding these two contradictory theories have been, since the Reformation, members of the English Church. It is none the less true, as Dr. Knox continually insists, that they represent entirely different religions. Their positions are mutually destructive. If the assertions on the one side are true, the assertions on the other are false. The antagonism has grown clearer as time has gone on and as the influence of Tractarianism has spread from the universities to the villages, the suburbs and the slums. It is even emphasized by the concessions and compromises of the Deposited Prayer Book, the main purpose of which is permanently to secure Stanley's comprehensiveness. But an all-embracing comprehensiveness is no longer regarded as possible. Although sometimes a bishop and sometimes a dean patronizingly appear on Nonconformist platforms and Nonconformist ministers are invited to preach on occasion in two or three English cathedrals, even the most persistent of the Protestants in the English Church would hesitate to imitate the dean who gave Holy Communion to a Unitarian Minister in Westminster Abbey. The negotiations initiated at Lambeth for the recognition of the schismatic sects have entirely and hopelessly broken down, owing mainly to the honest common sense of the Nonconformist leaders, who obstinately persist in believing that words mean what they say. There is therefore at this time no chance, so far as can be humanly judged, of the English Church becoming a really comprehensive national church, and unless the Catholic theory is accepted, it is merely one sect among many, given greater influence and importance by the fact of its association with the State.

Stanley naturally dreaded disestablishment because establishment emphasized Nationalism. His successors dread disestablishment because the Church for them has no splendour and dignity as the Catholic Church and, without bishops in the House of Lords and deans appointed by the Sovereign, it would lose colour and significance, and the meetings of ancient Convocations would have no greater importance than the annual assembly of the Congregational Union. What Erastian Churchman would care to wear the gaiters of the dean if the gaiters gave him no greater social importance than the frock-coat of the Wesleyan preacher round the corner?

This book is published at a critical moment in the history of a Church which passes from crisis to crisis with curious equanimity. The influence of the Tractarian movement is to be found written large in the Deposited Prayer Book – in the Prayers for the Dead, in the limited permission for the Reservation of the Blessed Sacrament, even in the new Canon of the Mass with its bias towards the belief in the Real Presence in the Sacrament of the Altar. But this half recognition, this half admission that Newman and Pusey and Keble were right when they contended that the English Church had never lost its Catholic character, is qualified by important concessions to Modernists – the Bishops have a proper regard for Dr. Inge's mordant pen – and by restrictions on the development of Catholic practice, if not of Catholic teaching. The book might have as its motto 'So far and no farther.' Its enactments will inevitably be resisted by men who, it was hoped, would be conciliated. It will bring not peace but a sharpened sword, and the old struggle between the two parties will go on and may become more bitter if the Bishops succeed in persuading Parliament to permit an Ecclesiastical Discipline Measure which will enable them to eject recalcitrant Catholic priests from their benefices.

This is what a vigorous prelate like Dr. Hensley Henson desires, and it is exactly what Stanley would oppose if he were alive to-day. It is true that out of friendship for Tait and in deference to Queen Victoria, he did not actively oppose the Public Worship Act, but he was acute enough to recognize, as Dr. Inge has recognized, that persecution does not pay and that the results are generally most unpleasant, not for the persecuted, but for the persecutor.

The Bishops' Book may be regarded as the last possible effort to keep the English Church partially comprehensive. It is doomed to failure. One of two things will result. Its restrictions may, as is anticipated by the more intelligent Evangelicals, damp down Catholic enthusiasm, prevent Catholic effort and reduce Anglo-Catholicism to the dull respectable level of Victorian High Churchism. It may be that the movement, begun ninety years ago, has reached its zenith and is now destined to dwindle into impotence. On the other hand if, despite the bishops, the movement continues to grow as it has grown during the last generation, backed by a wealth of scholarship at the Universities and inspired by the enthusiasm of hundreds of priests, particularly in slum parishes, sooner or later the little leaven must leaven the whole lump. Old-fashioned Protestantism has become so negligible in the Church that it has been entirely disregarded at the Lambeth Conferences and its leaders are the subjects of Dr. Henson's constant gibes. Modernism is a scholastic cult. It has no power to affect the lives of the commonplace world. No man was ever saved by a negation. The Erastian, eager for preferment and not too proud to intrigue for it, is still conspicuous among the clergy, though in these days he is inclined to be ashamed of himself. The Liberal Evangelical is for the moment dominant, but the dominance may not endure.

In this bewildering body, speaking, not with one voice, but with half a dozen, holding not one creed but half a dozen, following not one practice but at least twenty, Dr. Inge is a striking but hardly a typical figure. He is a modern Churchman in that he has small respect for the Church, but he has at least a higher regard for God than he has for man.

Each of my Deans has his outstanding qualities. In Colet they were enthusiasm and sympathy. I think of him, quiet and rather grave, sitting with Erasmus and Thomas More, eagerly listening to their talk of reform though hardly understanding their jokes and unable to join in their gay laughter. Donne was a gloomy mystic, hating himself and unable to escape from himself, loving God and unable to find Him. I think of him writing begging letters in his miserable house at Mitcham and in later years, when he had reached his deanery, bitterly recalling the excesses of his youth and particularly his truckling to the infamous Robert Carr. The gigantic Swift is a figure both for admiration and pity. Stanley, kind-hearted, bustling, limited, is, in his dignified respectability, by comparison a figure of mediocrity. It is too soon accurately to place Dr. Inge, but this may be said of him, that, looking out upon the world from the dome of St. Paul's, he finds it very bad.

FIVE DEANS

Tʜᴇ history of the Church militant is the history of its reformation. The instrument, designed for a divine purpose, has constantly grown blunted and has constantly needed grinding and sharpening. And at every crisis in the Church's long history the ultimate reformation has come from within. It has not been a case of conscience rebelling against authority, but of conscience quickened by authority. Pope Gregory VII was the outstanding reformer of the eleventh century, suppressing simony and insisting on a high standard of clerical conduct, and in the same century, Lanfranc came from Normandy to Canterbury to bring back order and spiritual enthusiasm to the Church in England. In the twelfth century, St. Bernard, the friend and adviser of a Pope, inspired the reform of the monastic life. St. Francis and St. Dominic were the great reformers of the thirteenth century, but they would have been powerless without the backing of supreme authority. The combination of spiritual fervour and the love of learning that distinguished the early sixteenth century was anticipated three hundred years before. The thirteenth century was the age of the founding of the great universities, and the new zeal for learning was closely connected with the new zeal for religion. St. Thomas Aquinas was a Dominican and Roger Bacon a Franciscan.

The century that followed was the darkest of all the eras in the Church's history. For seventy years the Popes resided at Avignon and the Papacy became, for the time, a national and not an international institution. There followed the schism of 1378 which for another fifty years made for confusion and paralysed activity. Reformation was again sorely needed, but authority was indifferent and the circumstances of the age excited rebellion. First John Wyclif and afterwards John Huss denounced the all too evident ecclesiastical abuses. They were both very able men, but unlike the earlier reformers, they acted not in collaboration with authority but in defiance of it, and it is remarkable that, again unlike the earlier and loyal reformers, they affected the life of the Church hardly at all. Huss was an extreme nationalist and undoubtedly a heretic, in both respects anticipating the 'reformers' of the sixteenth century. Wyclif was a rebel against the basic doctrines of the Catholic faith and, despite his vehement defence of the rascalities of his patron, John of Gaunt, something of a Socialist. To his followers the wearing of jewellery was as awful an evil as belief in the Mass. While the condition of the Church justified Wyclif's denunciation of prelates, it could not possibly justify his sudden denunciation of the doctrine of the Real Presence when he was fifty-one. The truth or untruth of Catholic teaching cannot be proved or disproved by the private lives of pontiffs or prelates. But men in all the ages have been indifferent to logic, and the greatest evil that has resulted from the occasional evil living of Church dignitaries has been that indignation, aroused by their misdeeds, has led to unphilosophic doubt concerning the assertions of the society of which the evil-doers were ministers. Because a bishop has a mistress, it is assumed by the unsophisticated that the sacraments can have no efficacy. Brilliant thinker and masterly prose writer as Wyclif was, he seems to have reasoned much in this way. He is rightly regarded as the forerunner of Luther and

16

Calvin. Like them he was an iconoclast. Like them he was the enemy not of the Church of Rome but of the Catholic religion.

It is improbable that Wyclif had much to do personally with the preparation of the Wyclif Bible, the first version of which was completed just before his death and the later version four years afterwards. This was the first complete translation of the Vulgate into English, but it must not be supposed that before Wyclif's time the Scriptures had been altogether out of reach of the simple man with no understanding of Latin. It should be remembered that, in the Middle Ages, every one who could read, could read Latin. Before the era of the printing press translations were not as necessary as they are today. There were, however, various translations of parts of Holy Scripture into Anglo-Saxon, and in the fourteenth century, and before Wyclif, the whole of the New Testament had been translated into English with the hearty approval of the Church. On the Continent the first thing that the printer did when he set up his first press was to print the Bible in the vernacular, and before the accession of Henry VIII such translations had appeared in France, Spain, Italy, Bohemia and Holland, while in Germany the Scriptures had been printed seventeen times before Luther's revolt. The claim that the Reformation gave back the Bible to the people is ridiculous. The Church has never had any desire to keep the Bible from the commonalty, although it has always most properly insisted that the Scriptures should be interpreted by authority and learning. In the thirteenth century, for example, Bishop Grosseteste ordered that Oxford students should devote the morning to the study of the Bible.

'Skilful builders,' he said, 'are always careful that foundation stones shall be really capable of supporting the building.' It is true that in the fifteenth century formalism and a decadent scholasticism had made Bible study in the University a tiresome formality, while, on the other hand, the Wyclif Bible with its occasional interpolation of extraneous and heretical matter was not unnaturally banned by the Church, particularly as Wyclif had taught that the Bible had an authority not only greater than that of the Church, but opposed to it. Lollardy had a certain popular vogue for a few years only. It had ceased to have any real influence in England before the dawn of the Renaissance, and the popular dislike of the Lollards is shown by the speech of Chaucer's shipman in the Prologue to the *Canterbury Tales*.

Sad as was the condition of the Church during the fourteenth and fifteenth centuries, there were rays of light in the darkness. Thomas à Kempis lived through the years of the schism in his poor monastery at Mount St. Agnes, simple in all worldly affairs, writing the immortal Imitation. Dante, the supreme artist of the Middle Ages, lived in the century of the Franciscans and the century of the schism. Chaucer has shown us that England was as laughter-loving in the fourteenth century as Dickens found it in the nineteenth, in circumstances almost as materialist and gloomy. St. Joan, the gallant mystic, brought back to her despairing fellow-countrymen the realization of the chivalry of goodness at the end of the schism, and died a martyr in 1431, in the midst of the confusion caused by protracted disunion. In these dark generations, too, the Popes were often men of light and learning. Clement VI boldly condemned moral offenders in high places and equally boldly succoured the victims of the plague. Innocent VI, the friend of Petrarch, was a genuine reformer and a notably successful peacemaker. Urban V was another reformer, a man of outstanding humility, properly beatified some fifty years ago. Gregory XI, who issued bulls against Wyclif, was equally busy with monastic reforms. There were sufficient abuses in the Church, but with them conspicuous piety and devotion.

Constantinople was captured by the Turks in 1453, during the pontificate of Nicholas V, a high-minded prelate of vast learning who founded a great library in Rome, was eager to stimulate the growth of Italian culture and may be properly regarded as the pioneer of the revival of learning. The half-century that followed was marked by stupendous achievement. Vasco da Gama sailed round the Cape of Good Hope in 1497 and Columbus reached America in 1492. The fifty years saw the production of the masterpieces of Da Vinci and Botticelli and the births of Michael Angelo and Raphael. Printing presses, first seen at Mainz in 1442, were set up in all the great European cities. And towards the end of the century, compensation for the fall of Constantinople was found in the expulsion of the Moors from Spain.

The Greek refugees from Constantinople taught Italy their language, almost unknown in western Europe a few years before, and stimulated interest in Greek philosophy. In the school in Florence, founded by Lorenzo de Medici, Plato was the rival of Christ, and with a widespread interest in culture and a passionate love of beauty there began an age of luxury unparalleled since the fall of the Roman Empire. The magnificence of the Medicis in

Florence was imitated in Rome and the Renaissance Popes were in effect luxurious secular princes surrounded by greedy place-hunting relatives. As Bishop Creighton has said: 'From the time of Sixtus IV nepotism was elevated into a political principle.' The paganizing of Italy may be realized by comparing the frescoes of Fra Angelico in San Marco in Florence with the pictures of Botticelli.

In Rome, the early Renaissance was seen at its worst; in Florence it was at its most attractive. Lorenzo the Magnificent, grandson of the shrewd banker Cosimo, was the tyrant of romance and the most picturesque product of money-lending that the world has ever known. He was cultured, generous, kindly, sufficiently a statesman to have become the most important personage in Italy, lavish in his patronage of literature, acute in his management of the Florentines whose liberty his family had destroyed. Under his rule, Florence was another Athens where Aristotle was regarded as almost divine and where the cult of the classic poets had replaced the cult of the saints, and cameos and ancient medals were valued far above the most sacred of relics. But at the very zenith of his greatness, Lorenzo and all that he represented were challenged, boldly, violently, crudely, by a black-haired Dominican friar, a man of small, undistinguished stature, whose deep-set eyes flashed under heavy brows and whose strong wide mouth told of indomitable firmness of purpose. It was in 1490, two years before Lorenzo's death, that Savonarola began to draw all Florence by his 'terrible sermons.' He was both a child of the Renaissance and a rebel against it. Gobineau puts into Savonarola's mouth a remarkable speech summarizing the meaning and inspiration of his mission. I quote it at length: —

'All is changing in our present epoch, already so different from the ages that have gone before; all is in froth and ferment; from a fresh centre, with a fresh horizon, will the universe henceforth unfold to us its sights. It will make for good if religion raises the cross; it will make for evil if the ever-active efforts of the wicked uproot and overthrow this tree of shelter. See you not what is coming to pass. Counterfeit sages are rising up and tearing from the walls the musty and worn-out tapestry that delighted former ages. Italy is full to bursting of unbridled adventurers, of upstart princes, of hireling soldiers, of tyrants of cities, despots of castles, rebel peasants, quarrelsome burgesses, and all inheritances great and small are the prey of this rabble, joined by the wolves that come to us in packs from Spain and France. And for all that, in the midst of these disasters, see what is happening! The nations are awakening; they rub their eyes; for their morning meal these famished creatures demand liberty and peace; liberty, I tell you, and above all the peace and the justice whereof their fathers never knew or tasted the savour. And I, I call to them: "Ask, above all, for faith!" Without faith, the rest is tasteless and turns to poison. But faith, where is it? Where shall we find its source again? The clergy reck naught of it. . . . The cardinals rend it. . . . The Pope . . . ah, the Pope! . . . I will not tell you what he is, you know too well! If we do not take care, there will issue from our unhappy Church, overgrown with brambles, from our rotting doctrines, from our decaying disciplines, the hideous heads of heresies, hissing from the tips of their forked tongues the excuses, the pretexts furnished them by these abominable doctrines, and turning them to venom. Do you mark them, these monsters seeking their quarry throughout the kingdoms of Christendom? And they have only too powerful an aid in those other vipers, the scholars, drunk with the pride of having learned to read in the new-found books of Greece and Rome. Do you not hear what counsellors they offer us, to take the place of the great doctors of theology? Plato, Seneca, the wretched Martial, the obscene Ovid, the impure Anacreon, a Lucan, a Petronius, a Statius, a Bion, an Apuleius, a Catullus. Every day you may see old greybeards, mad as the foolishest of youths, uttering these cries with a shameful enthusiasm and putting forward a page of Cicero as preferable to the holiest verses of our Gospels! Are these dangerous attacks enough, threats enough for the balance of men's consciences? No! The brush comes to join the pen, and with the brush the chisel and the engraver's tool, to reveal the new world to the eyes of a crowd amazed with infamous novelties. Yes, I say, all the senses of mind and heart are set in motion, stirred up, tickled by Satan; and if we must defend ourselves, it is high time to think of defence. Have you never heard tell of what they call "love of art" – which is really nothing but the shameful appetite for vice? This abomination has crept into our churches, which have thus become, what? – synagogues of the Devil! A Magdalene, a Sebastien, are only pretexts for unveiling the human form as shamelessly as Apollo and Venus. And I, I, who see and touch and feel and understand the horror of these degradations, I whose soul rises to furious disgust, yes, to the holy rage of indignation for the Cross, do you expect me to let these foulnesses heap their filth upon hapless humanity, without setting my life as a barrier against such an invasion? No! a thousand times no! I shall not remain inactive before such a levy of the forces of the archfiend! I shall defend the world! I shall defend the age in which I live!'

Gobineau, to whom Cesare Borgia was something of a hero, naturally had little sympathy with Savonarola, but he does not actually misrepresent him. The world was reawakening. It had to awaken to justice, liberty and decency, or to cruelty and lust. Savonarola's teaching was the reaction against the paganism of the Renaissance. Gobineau makes him denounce the beauties of art with the true Puritan's frenzy. But in Florence vice and tyranny had sheltered behind the artist, and even Gobineau's sentences, intentionally exaggerated, are not altogether unjustified. And as a matter of fact, Savonarola, for all his Puritan antics during the short theocracy that he established in Florence, cared both for learning and beauty. He founded schools for the teaching of craftsmanship and oriental languages and he saved a Medici Library from being sold, at the expense of the funds of the convent of San Marco. Above all, Savonarola cared for the poor as St. Francis had cared for them, and it was by the fearless flouting of tyrants that he won the people's ear. In 1495, Savonarola was the idol of the city. Michael Angelo, still a boy in his teens, listened to him in awe. Botticelli fled from Florence to escape from his influence, only to submit to it when the friar was beaten and deserted. The Medicis had been expelled. A semi-democratic government had been established, in which the friar's influence was paramount, with Machiavelli among its minor officials. Lorenzo's pagan Florence had become a Puritan Florence, though not for long. In his daily sermons Savonarola denounced the crimes of Alexander VI, the Borgia Pope, and he promptly refused the cardinal's hat offered him as a bribe for his silence. And for a while, backed by the loyalty of the city, he had nothing to fear.

In this year, 1495, Savonarola was concerned to prove in his sermons that denunciation of the wrongdoing of a Pope was not inconsistent with fealty to the Papacy, and among his congregation was a young Englishman of twenty-eight, eager and eminently serious, who after the sermons were delivered sought out the preacher in the pleasant monastery of San Marco and begged his counsel. The young Englishman was John Colet, the son of a rich London merchant and an ex-Lord Mayor who, like Savonarola himself, had chosen service in the Church rather than fortune in the city. Colet was born in 1467. He was educated at St. Anthony's School in London, and at Magdalen, Oxford, where More was among his fellow-undergraduates. In his journey to Italy, which had become the Mecca of the scholar, Colet was following the example set by Linacre, afterwards the founder of the College of Physicians, and Grocyn, who was to teach Greek to Erasmus, both of them his life-long friends. The influence of Colet's city father is shown by the fact that before he left Oxford and while he was still in minor orders, he was the non-resident rector of Dennington, Suffolk, the non-resident rector of Thurning, Huntingdonshire, and the non-resident vicar of the rich living of St. Dunstan's, Stepney. He was a living example of perhaps the greatest ecclesiastical evil of the time. The elder Colet, however much he may have deplored his son's determination to be a priest, had taken care that he should not be a poor priest. It seems quite clear that Savonarola had a great and fundamental effect on Colet at a most impressionable time in his life and through him on his fellows of the pre-Reformation humanist movement. Colet himself was never concerned in public affairs, but there is in his sermons a constant recognition that the Church's mission is mainly to the poor and unregarded, and it is probable that he often talked to Thomas More of the teaching of the Italian Dominican. Certainly the influence of the Florentine is very evident in the *Utopia*. The most important part of Savonarola's formula of government was the promotion of the public welfare at the expense of private interests, and the first thing to which he set his hand, when he became the practical ruler of Florence, was to find work for the unemployed, to secure the workers adequate wages and to ensure equal justice for all men. And all this is secured in More's *Utopia*. Savonarola's reign in Florence was short and ended in tragedy and apparent failure. But if, as has been said, 'the heart of the new learning is to be found in More's famous book,' then it was the politics of the new learning which Savonarola attempted to put into practice in Florence. The new learning was humanist and carried with it a revolt against inequality and injustice, and Savonarola did not fail because he was democratic before his time or because the forces of tyranny and injustice were too strong for him, but because he attempted to compel a pleasure-loving people to an unnatural austerity. The point of chief importance is that in the revolutionary and tumultuous sixteenth century, it was the men within the Church who, with all their consciousness of evils and abuses, never wavered in their fealty, who cared for the poor and denounced the tyrant, while the men who rebelled against the Church and separated themselves from it were not merely indifferent to the sufferings of the unfortunate, but were the eager allies of the oppressor. Savonarola thundered against cruelty, More indicted the social conditions of his age, Luther defended the massacre of revolting German peasants.

It was with religion and not with politics that Colet was concerned. In the autumn of 1495 he was back at Oxford arranging to deliver the series of lectures on the Epistles of St. Paul, which were to the Oxford Movement of the sixteenth century what Keble's Assize sermon was to the Oxford Movement of the nineteenth. The lecturer had no academic distinction, and it says a great deal for the open-mindedness of pre-Reformation Oxford, that the lectures were permitted and largely attended. But Oxford has always been the home of new causes. Though Colet may not have spoken as one having authority, he certainly did not speak as an unequipped scribe. He had studied Plato and Plotinus and he had a special enthusiasm for Cicero. He had read the Fathers and had already adopted the anti-Augustinian attitude that characterized all his teaching. Origen and Jerome attracted him. He was moved by the mystic writings of Dionysius and exasperated by the schoolmen, equally by St. Thomas Aquinas and Dun Scotus. He had prepared himself for his work as a preacher by reading every English book available to him. And during his two years on the Continent, and probably as the result of Savonarola's sermons, it was the Bible that had attracted him most of all.

The young scholar, dour, detached, keenly observant, learned many things during his foreign tour. With all the youth of his time, he felt himself the child of a golden age. The world was being reborn! But in the Rome of the Borgias he had seen that the new life could be more horrible than the old sleep, and in Florence he had listened to bitter prophecies of woe. The devil had captured the new tunes. The Church had failed to recognize the possibilities of the new age. While there was life in the world, there was dry rot in the Church. Nevertheless the Church remained a divine institution with a divine mission. And Colet dreamed of making the Church again effective as a means of grace by throwing open its windows, dragging down its fusty hangings and putting them into the dustbin and sweeping out its aisles and its sanctuaries. The Blessed Sacrament must remain on the altar, but there must be sunlight on the pulpit.

The Oxford lectures were realistic. In the fifteenth century, lectures on Holy Scriptures were usually textarian and pedantic, with the general idea that every text meant something that it did not say. The lecturers were concerned with allegory and double meanings. And it is noteworthy that the belief in verbal inspiration led then, as it has led since, to a complete loss of the spirit.

Colet described St. Paul's Epistles, probably to the rather shocked amazement of part of his audience, as the very human letters of a very human writer, and he proceeded to examine them, to make clear exactly what St. Paul meant and what is the implication of his teaching. It was particularly the love of God on which the lecturer insisted. 'When we speak of men as drawn, called, justified and glorified by grace,' he says, 'we mean nothing else than that men love in return God who loves them.' All through the lectures, there is an emphasis on the

27

connection between faith and life, between belief and conduct, and since Colet was speaking to men mostly in Holy Orders or preparing for ordination, it was naturally with the conduct of priests that he was most concerned. St. Paul had urged Timothy 'to avoid avarice and to follow after justice, piety, faith, charity, patience and mercy,' and Colet added that priests of his time would do well to set such an example as this to their own parishioners. The manuscript of the lectures has happily been preserved. Over and over again there is the suggestion of the influence of Savonarola, and it was probably lucky for Colet that in his later life he was content to admonish and did not follow his teacher into the stormy waters of public affairs.

Colet's lectures may have been revolutionary, but they were certainly popular. Learned doctors and mitred abbots came time after time to hear him, attracted it may be at first by the novelty of his point of view. The middle-aged orthodox at the end of the fifteenth century were not horrified by novelty but were on the contrary immensely interested by Colet's humanizing of religion. The religious reformer indeed has never lacked encouragement from the dignitaries of the Church so long as he has been content to be a reformer and not to become a destroyer, to be a man eager to make the Church more efficient for the fulfilment of its mission and not a teacher of false doctrine. Doubtless, too, Colet's success was partly due to his capacity for clear expression. In one of his letters Erasmus says to him: —

'You say what you mean, and mean what you say. Your words have birth in your heart, not on your lips.

They follow your thoughts, instead of your thoughts being shaped by them. You have the happy art of expressing with ease what others can hardly express with the greatest labour.'

The lectures gave Colet a position of influence and authority. Priests consulted him on questions of difficulty and in the winter of 1496–7 he wrote many letters expounding and elaborating his theology. Colet was a Liberal. This is particularly noticeable in his explanation of the first chapters of Genesis. Moses, he says, was explaining great mysteries to simple men. The story of the creation is a summary written 'after the manner of a popular poet.' Here there is a striking anticipation of the view of the modern theologian, and however offensive such an attitude to the Pentateuch may have been to the Catholic orthodox of his own day – and there is no evidence that it caused them the smallest perturbation – it would certainly have caused Colet uncomfortable persecution had he lived in the England of the seventeenth century Puritans, and would have ensured him an untimely death had it been his misfortune to reside in Geneva in the days of Calvin.

It is necessary to emphasize the fundamental differences between Colet and the Oxford reformers, whom he influenced, and the Protestant leaders, whose revolt led to the construction of a new religion, incidentally characterized by the horrified rejection of the Liberalism that was the most important quality of the Oxford Movement of the early sixteenth century.

It is as ridiculous to describe Luther and Calvin and Knox as reformers of the Church as it would be to describe

Lenin as a reformer of the Czardom. Colet was the reformer. Luther was the destroyer. The reformer failed. The destroyer had a measure of success. But Colet was at least partially justified in the counter-Reformation, but only partially, for even after four hundred years his Liberal Catholicism has only a limited acceptance. Yet there was nothing original in his teaching. In the spirit in which he interpreted the Old Testament, Colet was returning to tradition. His description of Moses, for example, was anticipated by Origen, who calls him 'a good and pious poet.' The Bible was to Colet the textbook of religion. In his lectures and letters he is all the time concerned to accent its ethical intention. 'Moses,' he says, 'wrote as he did for the men of his time, at once to allure them and draw them on to the worship of God.'

To Colet the mission of the Church was to help men to lead good lives, and therefore be hotly denounced the lax living of the bishops and priests. But he certainly did not reject the essential Catholic doctrine of the sacrifice of the Mass and the sacrificial nature of the priesthood. Indeed Mr. Seebohm, who writes from a definite Protestant standpoint, admits that 'according to Colet priests act on behalf of God towards man,' and his wrath against the faithless priests was caused by his conviction of the sacredness of their calling. 'Oh the abominable impiety of those miserable priests,' he writes, 'of whom this age of ours contains a great multitude, who fear not to rush from the bosom of some foul harlot into the temple of the Church, to the altar of Christ, to the mysteries of God.' The last phrases could hardly have been used by a man who anticipated the Protestant view of the Holy Eucharist. Colet was Franciscan in his emphasis on the supreme power and importance of love. 'Ignorant love,' he said, 'has a thousand times more power than cold wisdom' — a notable saying in an age that had re-discovered Plato and was soon to acclaim Machiavelli. Another contrast between Colet and the 'reformers' is to be found in his rejection of the Augustinian teaching which was to be developed into the horrors of Calvinism.

In the summer of 1498, Erasmus came to Oxford. Colet had been vastly affected by the eager, enthusiastic Florentine Dominican. From him he had acquired his righteous indignation that, to quote Mr. J. H. Stone, the Roman Catholic historian, 'adultery, simony, usury, defiled the sanctuary.' He was ambitious to lead men to a life of righteousness, caring most for the poor and the oppressed. Now he was to come into intimate contact with another of the outstanding figures of the age, a man in every way a contrast to the Florentine friar. Savonarola cared for souls. Erasmus cared for books. His life, indeed, may be described as a pilgrimage from library to library. Savonarola was in deadly earnest. Erasmus was a master of irony and sometimes its slave, and where Savonarola stormed, he laughed. The world has sometimes been cleansed by laughter. Dickens, for example, laughed Mr. Bumble practically out of existence and did a great deal to laugh away imprisonment for debt. The abuses that no man will deny existed in the Church in the fifteenth century were certainly things for good men's tears. They were things, too, for a wise man's laughter. But perhaps neither Rabelais nor Erasmus laughed loudly enough, and it needed the excesses of the Reformation and the destruction of the unity of Europe before the Counter-Reformation could cleanse the Church. There is no necessity to labour the enormous difference that must have resulted in the subsequent history of Europe if Leo X, the friend of Erasmus, and a dilettante of good intent, had had something of the earnestness of purpose of Pius V, and if the counter-Reformation had come half a century earlier.

Erasmus has been entirely misrepresented by Protestant apologists. An ease-loving scholar he would, as has been well said, have been far more comfortable with Lorenzo de Medici than with Savonarola. Moreover, he was not only affronted by the excesses of the reformers and resentful at being linked with Luther, but never at any time did he countenance or encourage rebellion against the.Papacy. 'I have sought,' he wrote, 'to save the dignity of the Roman Pontiff, the honour of Catholic theology and the welfare of Christendom.' And in the same letter, 'I have not deviated in what I have written one hair's breadth from the Church's teaching.' Every one knew that doctrines had been introduced into the Church which had no real sanction, 'partly by custom, partly by obsequious canonists, partly by scholastic definitions, partly by the tricks and arts of secular sovereigns,' and it was the desire of Erasmus and his friends to remove these excrescences. And that was all. He assured Cardinal Campeggio that 'Erasmus has been and always will be a faithful subject of the Roman See,' and in a letter to Warham he said: 'I admit that the corruption of the Church required a drastic medicine, but drugs wrongly given make the sick man worse.' As time went on and Luther's position became more defined, Erasmus's opposition to him was more outspoken, but it was the irony of the situation that appealed to him. He could see a joke when no other of his contemporaries could see it.

Thus when he heard that Luther had married a wife, Erasmus said: 'Some call Lutherism a tragedy. I call it a comedy where the trouble ends in a wedding.'

The attitude of Erasmus to the Church and to the Papacy was shared by his friends, by Colet and More, by Archbishop Warham and Bishop Fisher. Of them, Colet was the most earnest reformer, but it never occurred to him, as it never occurred to Savonarola, that the cleansing of clerical corruption, which was so insistent a duty, entailed any revolt against the Holy See or against the constitution of the Catholic Church.

Erasmus had been brought to England by Lord Mountjoy – the mediæval scholar rarely lacked a patron – and, after a short stay in London where he met Thomas More, he made his way, alone and with no knowledge of English, to Oxford, where he had been told that he could learn the Greek, necessary for his life work. As an Austin canon, he was welcomed by the Prior of the Augustinian college of St. Mary the Virgin, who introduced him to Colet, now a considerable university figure. Colet did not make friends easily, but Erasmus was irresistible and soon the two scholars became intimate. Erasmus, who was generally happy in England, liked and admired Colet and, with all the rest of the world, loved More and, in the manner of his age, he was effusively grateful for the patronage of Archbishop Warham, but there is more than a suggestion in the correspondence with Colet and in the record of their conversations that the great Dutchman was sometimes a little bored by the dour Londoner. Their intimacy was not in the least affected by the fact that Erasmus was a penniless scholar and Colet was well-to-do. But the two men were vastly different in character and

c

temperament, the one witty and vivacious, the other simple-minded and sometimes fiercely passionate. At Oxford they argued and almost wrangled. At first Erasmus was shocked by Colet's contempt for St. Thomas Aquinas and the schoolmen, but the Dutchman of genius became, to an extent, the pupil of the Englishman of talent – genius often learns from talent – and before he left Oxford, Erasmus had partially adopted Colet's rather dangerous formula: 'Keep to the Bible and the Apostles' Creed and let divines if they like dispute about the rest.' Colet tried to persuade Erasmus to stay on in Oxford and to supplement his own lectures on the Pauline epistles with similar lectures on the Old Testament. Erasmus protested that he had no equipment for such work. Perhaps, too, as Mr. Allen suggests, he had found the teaching of Greek at Oxford unsatisfactory. Anyhow he longed for Italy, though he afterwards admitted that he knew more Greek and Latin when he went to Italy than when he returned. He left Oxford in January, 1500, spent a few days with More in London and sailed from Dover on the 29th.

For five years longer Colet remained at Oxford, continuing each term his lectures on St. Paul. In 1504 he was given his doctorate and, thanks to the friendship of Archbishop Warham, appointed to the deanery of St. Paul's. His predecessor had commended himself to the city fathers by a jovial manner and a good table, and they must have been unpleasantly astonished to find the son of an ex-Lord Mayor frugal and ascetic, always soberly dressed, intent, when he entertained guests, more on improving conversation than on an elaborate menu; such a churchman, indeed, as the world, not unnaturally, has always found a little tiresome. As a secular priest and the dean of a great cathedral, with responsibilities to his colleagues and necessary intimacy with the citizens, Colet overdid austerity as other deans have overdone conviviality. He was a one-sided man. He understood the need for the fast, but in his life there was no place for the feast. And it was unfortunate that he should have held a position where, as Dean Hook says, 'hospitality was a decanal virtue, not to be dispensed with.' The Dean goes on: —

'The word "hospitality" in the middle age had a more extensive signification than it has at the present time. The dean and each member of the chapter had to provide, at his own expense, a common table for the members of the establishment of every degree. This was indeed the remuneration of the subordinate members of the corporation. At first, a common fund was established; but this fund was in process of time broken up, — the members of the chapter received dividends, and the inferior officer stipends. Still the custom of keeping hospitality lingered in many cathedrals, and in a modified state remained to our own times. Each dean and prebendary during his residence kept a certain number of public days; this was especially the case in Durham. In Colet's time, hospitality was in a transition state. The various officers of St. Paul's Cathedral received their salaries, and they expected the dean to keep a table for them, if not, as in times past, every day, yet probably on every festival of the Church, at a time when festivals were numerous. We can easily understand how these entertainments in London, among the lower class of the clergy and their dependents, degenerated into riotous living, and brought discredit on religion. The austere dean determined to effect a

35

reform. The munificence of the founder of St. Paul's
School was such as to secure him from the suspicion of
penuriousness, and Colet acted probably with the full
approbation of Warham and the higher ranks of the
clergy. It is not precisely what you do that gives offence,
but an unhappy manner of doing it. Colet so conducted
his reform as to excite against himself the animosity of all
the underlings of his church. The dean found it more
difficult to contend with the Cretan bellies of his petty
canons, than to struggle against the Bœotian intellects of
his opponents at Oxford.'

A stone's throw from the deanery, in lodgings in the
Charterhouse, Colet found an old friend. After the brilliant beginning of a political career, Thomas More had
offended the king and had been obliged to retire from
public life. He was living in the Charterhouse with
William Lily, the Greek scholar, and these two men with
two others of his Oxford intimates, Grocyn and Linacre,
formed Colet's London circle. More was a constant
attendant at Colet's cathedral sermons and it is said, on
the flimsiest evidence, that Colet persuaded him against
taking vows and adopting the religious life. More had had
a disappointing love affair. He was unhappy and appre-
hensive, and he might well have thought of the cloister as a
means of escape, and it is possible that, realizing that he
had no real vocation, Colet urged him against precipitate
action. Anyhow the desire was not for long, for in 1505
More married Jane Colt.

Soon after his appointment to St. Paul's Colet received
a letter of congratulation from Erasmus, who sent him a
copy of his recently published *Enchiridion* which, he said,

he had written 'to display neither genius nor eloquence but simply for this — to counteract the vulgar error of those who think that religion consists in ceremonies and in more than Jewish observances while they neglect what really pertains to piety.' Colet must have found evidence of the effect of his Oxford teaching in a book which was almost at once translated from the Latin into English and other languages, and was an immense success all through Europe. How little it offended orthodox Catholics is shown in a letter from a Spanish ecclesiastic to Erasmus in which the writer says that the *Enchiridion* 'has gained such applause and credit to your name and has proved so useful to the Christian faith that there is no other book of our time to be compared with it for the extent of its circulation since it is found in everybody's hands.'

Erasmus himself arrived in England for the second time in the winter of 1506, staying with More and paying a visit to Archbishop Warham, who was to be his gracious and understanding patron. Warham was a great and most attractive man. With greater enterprise than that of St. Thomas of Canterbury, he had obeyed the king's will and was both Chancellor and Primate, and he contrived to hold both offices under two monarchs for fifteen years. He was capable, modest, pious, simple in his life, the constant sympathetic friend of scholars and not a mere patronizing Mæcenas as Wolsey loved to be. It is the tragedy of the sixteenth century that Warham was overshadowed by Wolsey as Colet was overshadowed by Luther. When he died, an old man of over eighty, it was said of him: —

'And for the person of Bisshop of Canterbury ye may say ther canne be no person in Christendome more indifferente, more miet, apt, and convenient then the sayd archbisshop, who hath lernyng, excellent high and long experience, a man ever of a singular zele to justice.'

This second visit of Erasmus to England must have been extremely pleasant. When he returned to Paris in the summer of 1506 he wrote to Colet: —

'This I can say truly, that there is no whole country which has found me friends so numerous, so sincere, so learned, obliging, so noble and accomplished in every way, as the one City of London has done. Each has vied with others in affection and good offices, that I cannot tell whom to prefer. I am obliged to love all of them alike. The absence of these must needs be painful; but I take heart again in the recollection of the past, keeping them as continually in mind as if they were present, and hoping that it may so turn out that I may shortly return to them, never again to leave them till death shall part us. I trust to you, with my other friends, to do your best for the sake of your love and interest for me to bring this about as soon and as propitiously as you can.'

Henry VII died in 1509, and on April 23 Henry VIII was proclaimed king. Few events in history have been so universally regarded as the beginning of a new and happier age. The old king was a hard tyrant. His minions, the notorious Empson and Dudley, had been execrated. The new king was just eighteen, handsome, generous, the patron of learning, a child of the Renaissance. And with his by no means inconsiderable scholarship, there was a piety that must have persuaded Colet and his friends that in him the nation would find, in

Froude's phrase, 'a new Alfred or a Charlemagne.' More, anticipating the modern poet laureate, wrote a set of congratulatory verses on the king's accession and was appointed under-Sheriff of the City. Linacre became the king's physician. Warham retained his dual office. Erasmus hurried back from Rome to rejoin his friends, bringing with him the manuscript of the famous *In Praise of Folly*.

He stayed again with More at his house at Chelsea and in 1511 he was made Professor of Greek at Cambridge by John Fisher, then the university's chancellor, afterwards to be Bishop of Rochester and one of the Tudor martyrs. The lives and characters of Warham and Fisher are alone sufficient to prove the exaggeration of the wholesale abuse of the Church immediately before the Reformation. Erasmus was not happy at Cambridge. He complained of the lack of pupils. He complained of his loneliness. He complained of the quality of the beer. And after five years he returned to Flanders.

Meanwhile, in 1510, Colet had founded St. Paul's School. He had inherited a considerable fortune from his father, his personal expenses were of the smallest, and he resolved to spend his patrimony in establishing a school 'specially to increase knowledge and worshipping of God and our Lord Jesus Christ and good Christian life and manners in the children.' The intention summarizes the man, with his Erasmus-like zeal for learning and his Savonarola zeal for religion. Colet was conspicuous for his love of children and he had a rare understanding of 'the tenderness of little minds.' In the preface to the Latin grammar that he had prepared for his school he wrote: —

'I pray God all may be to his honour, and to the erudition and profit of children, my countrymen *Londoners* specially, whom, digesting this little work, I had always before mine eyes, considering more what was for *them* than to show any great cunning; willing to speak the things often before spoken, in such manner as gladly young beginners and tender wits might take and conceive. Wherefore I pray you, all little babes, all little children, learn gladly this little treatise, and commend it diligently unto your memories, trusting of this beginning that ye shall proceed and grow to perfect literature, and come at the last to be *great clerks*. *And lift up your little white hands for me*, which prayeth for you to God, to whom be all honour and imperial majesty and glory. Amen.'

A school-house was built for the accommodation of one hundred and fifty-three boys in St. Paul's Churchyard, and Lily, who had learned Greek in Rhodes, was appointed first head master at a very generous salary. Colet had consulted Erasmus about the masters for his school, and in reply Erasmus sent him a letter in which he suggested the necessary scholastic qualifications: —

'In order that the teacher might be thoroughly up to his work, he should not merely be a master of one particular branch of study. He should himself have travelled through the whole circle of knowledge. In philosophy he should have studied Plato and Aristotle, Theophrastus and Plotinus; in Theology the Sacred Scriptures, and after them Origen, Chrysostom, and Basil among the Greek fathers, and Ambrose and Jerome among the Latin fathers; among the poets, Homer and Ovid; in geography, which is very important in the study of history, Pom-

ponius Mela, Ptolemy, Pliny, Strabo. He should know
what ancient names of rivers, mountains, countries, cities,
answer to the modern ones; and the same of trees, animals,
instruments, clothes, and gems, with regard to which it is
incredible how ignorant even educated men are. He
should take note of little facts about agriculture, architecture, military and culinary arts, mentioned by different
authors. He should be able to trace the origin of words,
their gradual corruption in the languages of Constantinople, Italy, Spain, and France. Nothing should be
beneath his observation which can illustrate history or
the meaning of the poets. But you will say what a load
you are putting on the back of the poor teacher! It is so;
but I burden the one to relieve the many. I want the
teacher to have traversed the whole range of knowledge,
that it may spare each of his scholars doing it. A diligent
and thoroughly competent master might give boys a fair
proficiency in both Latin and Greek, in a shorter time and
with less labour than the common run of pedagogues take
to teach their babble.'

It may be suggested that few public schoolmasters
nowadays would satisfy Erasmus.

By the king's command the Archbishop summoned
Convocation to meet in St. Paul's in February, 1512, and
the Dean was appointed to preach the opening sermon.
This sermon was delivered in Latin, as it would be now,
and as were Colet's Oxford lectures, though he habitually
preached in his cathedral in English. Latin was a very
live language in the early days of the reign of Henry
VIII. It is said that Erasmus never learned to speak
either English or Italian and that he almost forgot his

native Dutch. He spoke and wrote and thought in Latin, which was still the *lingua franca* of the educated. More's *Utopia* was, of course, written in Latin.

The nominal purpose for which Convocation was called was the extirpation of heresy, and it is true that there had been several prosecutions of Lollards for heresy since Henry's accession and that two of them had been burned at Smithfield. The obvious exaggeration of the persecution is due to a joke made by Ammonius, the king's Latin secretary, in a letter to Erasmus in which he complained that wood was scarce because 'the heretics cause so many holocausts.' It would seem, however, from Colet's very long sermon, that Convocation was expected to inquire into the general state of the Church. Not one word did he say of heretics or heresy, and this is the more striking since, according to Foxe, Colet was one of the judges appointed by the Bishop of London to try the accused Lollards.

In forcible and eloquent language, Colet denounced clerical abuses in the familiar Renaissance manner, and urged the need for reformation. 'Do you, spiritual doctors,' he said, 'first essay that medicine for the purgation of morals, and then you may offer it to us to taste of it also.' There was no necessity for new legislation. 'The need is not for the enactment of new laws and constitutions but for the observance of those already enacted.' Men should not be rashly admitted to Holy Orders. Preferment should be the reward of merit. Simony should be stamped out. Incumbents should live in their parishes and bishops in their dioceses, and Colet showed how completely Catholic he remained by including among the duties of bishops 'that they sacrifice for their people.' The ecclesiastical courts should be reformed and 'Provincial Councils should be held more often for the reformation of the Church, for nothing ever happens more detrimental to the Church of Christ than the omission of Councils both general and provincial.' This insistence on the importance of Provincial Councils and on the principle of synodical government is particularly notable and interesting at a time when one English Diocesan after the other has summoned a Sacred Synod in order to obtain approval for much discussed proposals of great and outstanding significance. Bishops and priests must set an example of goodness and piety. 'First rule well, and labour in word and doctrine and then the people will hold you in all honour.' The preacher agreed that clerks should not be 'drawn before civil courts' but they must be worthy of their privileges.

Archbishop Warham must have had a shrewd idea of the sort of sermon that Colet was likely to preach, but it is not surprising that some of the older and stupider prelates were furious. It was difficult with any decency directly to complain of the Convocation sermon, but Colet was accused of having taught, in certain of his other sermons in St. Paul's, that images should not be venerated, of having made a direct attack on his diocesan in a reference to divines who read their sermons, and of having misinterpreted the admonition addressed to St. Peter, 'Feed my lambs,' in applying it to the incomes of the bishops. St. Peter had no money, the Dean's enemies asserted, and therefore the feeding in our Lord's mind must have been spiritual. Warham treated the charges with the contempt that they deserved and Colet was mildly amused, as he was when his school was described as a 'temple of idolatry.' Tyndall says that he was also accused of heresy for translating the Paternoster into English, but this is most improbable and almost certainly untrue. The whole thing was a storm in a tea cup, the result of that not uncommon occurrence, an old Conservative bishop resenting the zeal of a younger man's enthusiasm. Colet went on with his school and his preaching and Erasmus wrote him the following letter of congratulation from Cambridge: —

'I was delighted to hear from you and have to congratulate you that you have returned to your most sacred and useful work of preaching. I fancy even this little interruption will be overruled for good, for your people will listen to your voice all the more eagerly for having been deprived of it for a while. May Jesus, *Optimus Maximus*, keep you in safety!'

Henry VIII soon disappointed the hopes of his admirers. They had anticipated an era of peace and brotherhood. The king had confirmed their hopes by his prompt and proper punishment of Empson and Dudley, his father's extortioners. But he was young and eager to play a great part in the world, and young ambitious princes are apt to dream of war. Reform was swamped by imperialism, as it always is. In 1512 Henry sent a pathetically futile expedition to France. The next year he fitted out a great fleet, which did nothing ingloriously, and he himself led a second army across the Channel which won the farcical Battle of the Spurs and then, after many marchings and joustings, the king came home. It should be added that he was the enemy of France because his wife was the daughter of the Emperor and because the vile game of the balance of power had already begun. During the king's absence the Battle of Flodden had been won on the Scottish frontier. And with it ended the military history of the eighth Henry. Colet and his friends bitterly attacked the war spirit. Erasmus wrote: –

'The wars of Christian princes begin for the most part either out of ambition or hatred or lust, or like diseases of the mind. Consider also by whom they are carried on: by homicides, by outcasts, by gamblers, by ravishers, by the most sordid mercenary troops, who care more for a little pay than for their lives. These offscourings of mankind are to be received into your territory and your cities that you may carry on war. Think, too, of the crimes which are committed under pretext of war, for amid the din of arms good laws are silent; what rapine, what sacrilege, what other crimes of which decency forbids the mention!

Colet was bolder still. He spoke out before the king himself in a sermon preached on Good Friday, 1513. Henry, who was still kindly and chivalrous, listened patiently if he did not heed. A few days afterwards he had a long conversation with the dean at Greenwich and when Colet had gone, he said to the courtiers who expected his disgrace: 'Let every man have his own doctor, and let every one favour his own. This man is the doctor for me.' But Wolsey's star was rising, and the hopes of the little group of reformers and genuine patriots were growing fainter.

In 1515 Warham, who shared his friend's dislike of Henry's 'spirited foreign policy,' and was particularly opposed to war with France, resigned the Chancellorship to Wolsey. He was sixty-five, and for those days an old man, though he was to live for another seventeen years, and he was eager for a quiet life and not unwilling to give way to his pushing, ambitious successor who, as Archbishop of York and Papal Legate, was practically the head of the Church in England. Wolsey was obsessed with foreign affairs and during his years of office gave little attention to the condition of England or to the affairs of the Church, though he professed sympathy with the would-be reformers of abuses. With the king and Wolsey benevolent, there is, however, every reason to believe that the Church in England would have gradually cleansed itself and grown more competent to fulfil its divine mission, without any forcible break in its Catholic tradition or without the subsequent semi-patronage of German excesses and heresies, had it not been for Henry's obstinate determination to go his own way, to flout the supreme spiritual authority and to outrage accepted Christian morality. The suggestion that the Reformation began in England with the sex vagaries of a lecherous king is often denounced as a cheap and ignorant gibe. As a matter of fact, it is entirely in accordance with the facts. Certainly there was no popular revolt against the teachings of the Catholic Church in England until the end of the reign of Mary, though there may have been – even of this there is small proof – popular resentment of the abuses which Colet denounced. The cleansed Church, however, of which Colet dreamed and for which More and Fisher died, was not to be, and if, as Erasmus suggested, Lutheranism was a comedy, Coletism was a tragedy.

The king was far more concerned with 'glory' than with the good of his people, who were exhausted by the taxation necessary to pay for the ridiculous French wars, and harassed by penal legislation designed in the interest of the landowners, who were finding it more and more profitable to breed sheep rather than to grow corn. The result was increased misery in the countryside, which was ravaged by the hordes of discharged soldiers, landless and desperate men. Colet, almost alone among the men of his time, really cared for the poor, and it was characteristic of him that he should have concluded his sermon in Westminster Abbey on November 18, 1515, on the occasion of Wolsey's installation as a Cardinal, with the admonition: 'My Lord Cardinal, be glad and enforce yourself always to do and execute righteousness to rich and poor with mercy and truth.'

A few months before, Colet was saddened by the departure of Erasmus for Basle. The two friends went together to the shrine of St. Thomas at Canterbury, and Erasmus has left a racy and maybe rather malicious account of the journey, Colet's utter want of humour obviously moving the philosopher to humorous exaggeration. Colet at least understood that St. Thomas shared his passion for the unhappy and the needy and, when he was shown the high altar piled with the gifts of the pious, soon to be stolen by that vulgar ruffian, Thomas Cromwell, he suggested that the saint would be far better pleased if the offerings had been sold and the money given to the poor. The relics, none too clean, that he was asked to kiss offended his fastidiousness, and he broke out into angry denunciation when an unfortunate beggar offered the leather of St. Thomas's shoe for his veneration, Erasmus laughingly soothing the beggar's wounded feelings. The incident, warmly applauded by Protestant historians, shows a want of imagination and sympathy in a man forced to an excessive realism by the circumstances of his time.

After eight months Erasmus returned to England for a short stay, having added to a new edition of his *Adagia*, a bitter attack on kings who wasted their money in wars when they might have subsidized the work of scholars. More's *Utopia* and Erasmus's *Novum Instrumentum*, his Greek Testament with a Latin translation, were both published in 1515, and Erasmus published his *Institutes of a Christian Prince* in 1516. The 'Institutes' suggests what might have happened in Europe if Erasmus and not Machiavelli had been the guides of the later Renaissance princes, and if, instead of adopting the Italian's narrow Paganism, they had heeded the precept of Erasmus: 'As often as it comes into your mind that you are a prince, call to mind that you are a Christian prince,' a prince that is who is 'useful to his people.' Erasmus sent copies of both his books to Colet, who said in his letter of acknowledgment: —

'What you say about the New Testament I can understand. The volumes of your new edition of it (the *Novum Instrumentum*) are here both eagerly bought and everywhere read. By many, your labours are received with approval and admiration. There are a few, also, who disapprove and carp at them, saying what was said in the letter of Martin Dorpius to you. But these are those divines whom you have described in your *Praise of Folly* and elsewhere, no less truly than wittily, as men whose praise is blame, and by whom it is an honour to be censured.

' For myself, I so love your work, and so clasp to my heart this new edition of yours, that it excites mingled feelings. For at one time I am seized with sorrow that I

48

have not that knowledge of Greek, without which one is good for nothing; at another time I rejoice in that light which you have shed forth from the sun of your genius.

'Indeed, Erasmus, I marvel at the fruitfulness of your mind, in the conception, production, and daily completion of so much, during a life so unsettled, and without the assistance of any larger and regular income.

'I am looking out for your *Jerome* who will owe much to you, and so shall *we* also when able to read him with your corrections and explanations.

'You have done well to write *De Institutione Principis Christiani.* I wish Christian princes would follow good institutes! By their madness everything is thrown into confusion. . . .

'As to the "peaceful resting-place" which you say you long for, I also wish for one for you, both peaceful and happy; both your age and your studies require it. I wish, too, that this your final resting-place may be with us, if you think us worthy of so great a man; but what we are you have often experienced. Still you have here some who love you exceedingly.'

The letter was written 'from the country at Stepney, with my mother, who still lives and wears her advancing age beautifully, often happily and joyfully speaking of you.' The note of appealing affection shows Colet in his most attractive aspect. In another letter to Erasmus, Colet complained that his friend sent messages to him through others instead of writing direct, and he concluded :—

'O Erasmus! of books and of knowledge there is no end. There is no thing better for us in this short life than to live holily and purely, and to make it our daily care to be purified and enlightened, and really to practise what these "Pythagorica" and "Cabalistica" of Reuchlin promise; but, in my opinion, there is no other way for us to attain this than by the earnest love and imitation of *Jesus*. Wherefore leaving these wandering paths, let us go the short way to work. I long, to the best of my ability, to do so. Farewell.'

In 1517 Tetzel was selling indulgences in Germany and Luther nailed his famous thesis to the church door in Wittenberg. The reformation had begun. The hopes of the humanist reformers were finally shattered. Europe was fated to be rent in twain. Erasmus was as indignant as Luther at the sale of indulgences. He wrote to Colet, 'What could be more shameless than these continued indulgences?' but he realized that the 'reformers' would perforce act 'to the detriment of us who are labouring to benefit mankind.' And Colet shared his friend's sorrow and disappointment.

His last years were uneventful, but very sad. In 1518 he had a severe attack of sweating sickness, which left him with a broken constitution. He was weary of endless conflict with his bishop. He longed to resign his deanery and to spend the rest of his life in remote retirement. We hear of him succouring unfortunate prisoners. And he carefully drew up the statutes by which his school was to be governed after his death. 'The most honest and faithful fellowship of the Mercers of London' were appointed governors of the school, 'married citizens of established reputation,' as Erasmus calls them, though I have not the smallest idea why he supposed that all honest and faithful mercers are necessarily married. From this selection perfervid Protestants have boldly assumed, with a singular logic, that Colet was opposed to clerical celibacy. It is true that he provided that his school might have married masters, and it is possible that he would have preferred that the masters should be laymen, but that does not prove that he would have preferred that priests should have wives.

The Statutes are a very large-minded document. Boys were not to be admitted to the school until they could read and write, but the curriculum was only stated in general terms and much was left to the discretion of future governors and masters, Colet 'exhorting them to fear the terrible judgment of God who seeth in darkness and shall render to every man according to his works; and finally praying the great Lord of mercy for their faithful dealing in this matter now and always to send unto them in this world much wealth and prosperity and after this life much joy and glory.' It was perfectly natural that the son of a Lord Mayor should have entrusted his creation to a City Company of which probably his father was a member, and to attach dogmatic importance to the selection is sheer nonsense.

Colet died on September 16, 1519, two years before Leo X gave Henry VIII the title of Defender of the Faith, ten years before the king fell in love with Anne Boleyn, eleven years before the fall of Wolsey, fifteen years before Henry was proclaimed the Head of the Church. He was saved from many things that his friends, More and Fisher and Warham, were fated to endure. 'What a man has England and what a friend have I lost,' wrote Erasmus when he heard of his death. And in another letter he wrote that Colet's name should be inscribed on the roll of the saints. The high regard of his contemporaries is

shown in a letter written to him a year before his death
by one of the canons of Mainz:—

'I have often thought with admiration of *your* blessedness, who born to wealth and of so illustrious a family
have added to these gifts of fortune manners and intellectual culture abundantly corresponding therewith. For
such is your learning, piety, and manner of life, such lastly
your Christian constancy, that notwithstanding all these
gifts of fortune, you seem to care for little but that you
may run in the path of Christ in so noble a spirit, that
you are not surpassed by any even of those who call themselves "mendicants." For they in many things simulate
and dissimulate for the sake of sensual pleasures.

'When recently the trumpet of cruel war sounded so
terribly, how did you hold up against it the image of
Christ, the olive-branch of peace! You exhorted us to
tolerance, to concord, to the yielding up of our goods for
the good of a brother, instead of invading one another's
rights. You told us that there was no cause of war between Christians, who are bound together by holy ties
in a love more than fraternal. And many other things of
a like nature did you urge, with so great authority, that I
may truly say that the virtue of Christ thus set forth by
Colet was seen from afar. And thus did you discomfit the
dark designs of your enemies. Men raging against the
truth, you conquered with the mildness of an apostle.
You opposed your gentleness to their insane violence.
Through your innocence, you escaped from any harm,
even though by their numbers (for there is always the
most abundant crop of what is bad) they were able to
override your better opinion. With a skill like that with

which Homer published the praises of Achilles, Erasmus has studiously held up to the admiration of the world and of posterity the name of England, and especially of Colet, whom he has so described that there is not a good man of any nation who does not honour you. I seem to myself to see that each of you owes much to the other, but which of the two owes most to the other I am doubtful. For he must have received good from you; seeing that you are hardly likely to have been magnified by his colouring pen. You, however, if I may freely say what I think, do seem to owe some thanks to him for making publicly known those virtues which before were unknown to us.'

John Colet stood for learning, piety and the Catholic faith, and he and his contemporaries proved their piety by their zeal for learning. I have already referred to the influence of Warham, the Chancellor of Oxford, and Fisher, the Chancellor of Cambridge. Foxe, Bishop of Winchester, founded Corpus Christi at Oxford, and Wolsey founded Cardinal's College, and Colet left his monument in St. Paul's School. With the break with Rome, the surrender to the German heresies and Cranmer's invitation to foreign Protestants to the Universities, learning in England rapidly declined. In the years 1547 and 1548 not one single degree was taken at Oxford, and so bad were things in Cambridge in 1545 that the speedy end of the University was anticipated.

Colet, says Dr. Inge, 'stands for a combination of Humanism and Christian austerity in morals, for Liberalism in theology combined with reverence for the great philosophical tradition.'

53

COLET died in 1519. John Donne became Dean of St. Paul's in 1621. Colet had dreamed of a Church reformed, eager, Catholic. But the Reformation had done everything except reform. The Church of the Elizabethan settlement, of which Donne was a dignitary, had cut itself adrift from Rome with certainly no obvious increase in moral fervour. It had grown completely indifferent to the poor and the oppressed. And professing to stand midway between Rome and Geneva, it claimed a Catholicity which was challenged and denied by the rest of the Catholic world.

Colet had come to London from a Catholic Oxford, at the beginning of the sixteenth century, enthusiastic for the new learning. But the new religion had swamped the new learning and, at the end of the century, Reformation Oxford cared nothing for scholarship or character, and its proctors and lesser officers were chosen merely for their ability to provide lavish entertainments. Pluralism and absenteeism were at least as flagrant in the Church as they had been before the Reformation, and clerical luxury had increased with the abolition of compulsory clerical celibacy. Cardwell says :—

'You will find deans usually in their velvet, damask or satin cassocks, with their silk netherstocks, nay some archdeacons and inferior ministers, having two benefices, are likewise for the most part so attired; to omit that their wives, in the cost and vanity of their apparel, do exceed as much more, which is one principal motive why there is such exclamation against double-beneficed men, and such as besides their two benefices have some other preferment *sine cura.*'

England was insular for the first time since the Norman Conquest. In the later years of the reign of Elizabeth and until the Puritan revolution, the Church of England was engaged in a bitter struggle with the extravagant extremists of the Reformation, against whom she contended without the aid of the spiritual zeal of the counter-Reformation. England, almost alone among European nations, gained nothing from the reforms of the three great counter-Reformation Popes, the Dominican Pius V, Gregory XIII, and the Franciscan Sixtus V. She had no share in the quickened faith that sent missions to America and the Far East. She was unaffected by the preaching of St. Francis de Sales and she did not hear the call to social service that came from St. Philip Neri and St. Vincent de Paul.

Decency and order in the Church were challenged by farcical fanatics like the author of the Martin Marprelate libels, who wrote of the Archbishop as the 'Beelzebub of Canterbury, the Canterbury Caiaphas, a monstrous anti-Christ, a most bloody tyrant.' Against such opponents the Church, bewildered, weakened, uncertain, endeavoured in a half-hearted way to establish its character as an integral part of the Church Catholic and to demonstrate the possibility of a non-Papal Catholicism. Before the end of the seventeenth century, the Church was saved from the Puritans, but only after years of struggle and persecution which brought with them the inevitable strengthening and reform and gave the Church of England notable saints and at least one martyr.

John Donne was not one of the saints. Like Colet, he was the son of a substantial London citizen. His father was a freeman of the City, and a member of the Ironmongers' Company. On his mother's side, he was descended from Elizabeth, the sister of Sir Thomas More. Both his father's and his mother's families had remained staunch to the old faith, despite the Elizabethan persecutions and cajoleries, and his mother's kinsmen – she herself is always described as 'a stubborn Papist' – had paid dearly for their fidelity. Donne's great-great-grandmother died in exile at Malines. His great-grandfather and great-grandmother died in exile at Louvain. His grandfather, John Heywood, narrowly escaped martyrdom, and also died at Malines; and his mother's two brothers, who were among the first Englishmen to join the Society of Jesus, died in exile. 'No family,' said Donne, 'which is not of far larger and greater branches hath endured and suffered more in their persons and fortunes for obeying the teachers of Roman doctrine.'

Donne was born in the parish of St. Nicholas Olave in 1573. His father died three years afterwards, leaving two baby sons and a daughter. Despite the disabilities, English Catholics at the end of the Elizabethan era still sent their sons to the Universities, though Catholic students avoided taking degrees in order that they might not be compelled to swear the oath of allegiance to the English Church. Donne went up to Oxford with his younger brother in 1584 when he was eleven, but apparently he only stopped at the university for two years. He may have feared sharing the fate of his uncle Jasper who, in 1585, had been arrested and banished. From Oxford, Donne went to Trinity, Cambridge, where he stayed until the end of 1589. Sir Edmund Gosse makes the interesting suggestion that Donne, who was precociously clever, was affected during his two years at Oxford by the Spanish mystics. Interest in everything Spanish had begun at the university with the marriage of Henry VIII with Catherine of Aragon, and continued to the Civil War, and it is possible that this Spanish cult, to which he would naturally be attracted, caused Donne to become acquainted while he was still a boy with the teaching of St. Theresa and St. John of the Cross.

When he was nineteen, he entered Lincoln's Inn. In the following year, 1593, a proscribed Roman seminarist was arrested in his brother's chambers at Thavies Inn. His brother himself was committed to the Clink prison, where he died of fever, and this incident appears to have convinced Donne of the wisdom of gravely considering the question of his own religion. He was a wealthy young man with many influential friends and the prospect of a pleasant life. But his prospects were certainly precarious so long as he continued loyal to the old faith. Izaak Walton, the first as well as the most charming and most enthusiastic of Donne's biographers, says that it was in 1593, the year of his brother's death, that Donne entered the Anglican Communion. Sir Edmund Gosse says that there is nothing to show that he became an Anglican until ten years later. The fact, however, remains that his conversion was entirely in accord with self-interest, while the retention of his father's faith entailed considerable danger and made exile a practical certainty. It is always hard to believe in the genuineness of a change of religion that is quite certain to pay, and there is something not a little contemptible in the haste with which John Donne, the descendant of generations of martyrs, joined the dominant Church. The meanness is not made any the less by the grandiloquence of his *Pseudo-Martyr*, written in 1610, in which he explains that conviction only came to him after much reading and prayer. Sir Edmund Gosse says that his attachment to the Catholic faith declined when he escaped from his mother's tutelage, and the eroticism of his early poems indicates a revolt against all religious restrictions far more than any intellectual aversion to Roman doctrine.

Donne bloomed early as a poet. His satires were written while he was in the early twenties. It might have been supposed that the young poet would have eagerly sought the friendship of the great Elizabethans who lived on into the reign of James. But Ben Jonson seems to have been his only friend among them. There is nothing to show that he ever met Shakespeare, and it is doubtful whether he ever entered the Mermaid. The religious pervert seems, indeed, to have been something of a snob.

When he was twenty-three, Donne went with the Earl of Essex and Sir Walter Raleigh on the expedition against Cadiz, and in 1597 he was again with Essex in the unsuccessful expedition to the Azores, being anxious, as he said, to escape for a while from London and from 'the queasey pain of being beloved and loving.' Essex sailed to the Azores in 1597, and Izaak Walton says that instead of returning to England, Donne spent years travelling in Italy and Spain, but Sir Edmund Gosse believes that his years on the Continent were between 1592 and 1596 and that Essex agreed to take him to the Azores because of his command of the Spanish language. As for his mode of living during these years, Sir Edmund Gosse says 'he was tasting life and rolling it, a savoury morsel, upon his tongue.'

The phases of Donne's life are all reflected in his poems. In his early twenties, he was in revolt. He had already ceased to believe the religion of his family, and rebellion

against the old faith encouraged rebellion against established fashion. It is true that the year 1593 when Donne's
earliest poem was written was – I quote Sir Edmund
Gosse – 'the central date of the luxuriant blossoming of
lyrical and dramatic, pastoral and amatory verse in England which has been the marvel and the bewilderment of
critics.' But already the Renaissance was drawing to that
end of disillusionment which finds its expression in 'The
Tempest.' With zenith there came reaction, reaction
against the sentimentalities and exaggerations proper to
the age of the Armada. Donne, the poet, was rebel against
both the mood and the conventions of the sixteenth
century, and despising to follow in the footsteps of
writers of established reputation, he was the chief of a
small group of English writers who first attempted to
acclimatize the satire in English literature. Horace,
Juvenal, and particularly Persius, were his masters. In
his four Satires he gibes at types and not at individuals.
The last Satire begins:–

'Away thou fondling motley humorist,
Leave me, and in this standing wooden chest,
Consorted with these few books, let me lie
In prison, and here be coffin'd, when I die;
Here are God's conduits, grave Divines; and here
Nature's Secretary, the Philosopher;
And jolly Statesmen, which teach how to tie
The sinews of a city's mystic body;
Here gathering Chroniclers, and by them stand
Giddy fantastic Poets of each land.'

The lines are strong and harsh and effective. The
Satire contains what is, I suggest, a sneer in execrable

taste at the religion of his family, but, remembering how dearly his family had paid for their religion, the reference in the second Satire to Roman Catholics as 'poor disarm'd not worth hate,' is even more unpleasant. Even Sir Edmund Gosse finds in this second Satire 'the ugly parts of the poet's genius, its arrogance, its truculence, its immodesty.' The Third Satire is a sneer at the religious man. At Rome there are only the rags of religion. At Geneva the poet finds

'Religion, plain, simple, sullen, young,
Contemptuous, yet unhandsome.'

The Church of England is young and far too comprehensive.

'Graius stays still at home here, and because
Some Preachers, vile ambitious bawds, and laws
Still new like fashions, bid him think that she
Which dwells with us, is only perfect, he
Embraceth her, whom his Godfathers will
Tender to him, being tender, as Wards still
Take such wives as their Guardians offer, or
Pay values.'

The poet himself professes to anticipate that tiresome Victorian bore, 'an honest doubter.' In a very fine passage he says:—

'On a huge hill,
Cragged and steep, Truth stands, and he that will
Reach her, about must and about must go,
And what the hill's suddenness resists, win so;
Yet strive so, that before age, death's twilight,
Thy soul rest, for none can work in that night.'

60

In the Fourth Satire there is evidence of Donne's wide reading and of the love of adventure which he shared with most of the men of his age and which caused him to sail with Essex and Raleigh. To these expeditions literature owes his two poems 'The Storm' and 'The Calm' in which the poet uses homely realistic imagery and avoids any attempt at over ornamentation. I quote the following from 'The Storm':—

'Then, like two mighty kings which, dwelling far
Asunder, meet against a third to war,
The south and west winds joined, and, as they blew,
Waves like a rolling trench before them threw.
Sooner than you read this line, did the gale,
Like shot not feared till felt, our sails assail,
And what at first was called a gust, the same
Hath now a storm's, anon a tempest's name.'

During the ten years before his marriage Donne wrote the love poetry which with its many other qualities is remarkable for a realism that is often brutal. In 'The Indifferent' he boldly proclaims his inconstancy:—

'I can love both fair and brown,
Her whom abundance melts, and her whom want betrays,
Her who loves loneness best, and her who masks and
    plays,
Her whom the country form'd and whom the town,
Her who believes, and her who tries,
Her who still weeps with spongy eyes,
And her who is dry cork, and never cries;
I can love her, and her, and you and you,
I can love any, so she be not true.'

And, of course, it is the inconstancy of woman that justifies the inconstancy of man: —

'If thou be born to strange sights,
　　Things invisible to see,
Ride ten thousand days and nights,
　　Till age snow white hairs on thee,
Thou, when thou return'st, wilt tell me
　　All strange wonders that befell thee,
　　　　And swear
　　　　No where
Lives a woman true, and fair.'

So inconstancy becomes a positive virtue.

'Let no man tell me such a one is fair,
And worthy all alone my love to share.
Nature in her hath done the liberal part
Of a kind Mistress, and employ'd her art
To make her loveable, and I aver
Him not humane that would turn back from her:
I love her well, and would, if need were, die
To do her service. But follows it that I
Must serve her only, when I may have choice
Of other beauties, and in change rejoice?'

From many loves Donne passed to one, to an unpleasant intrigue with the wife of an invalid, who apparently regarded Donne as his friend, a fact that did not prevent the poet from courting his mistress in her husband's home. He writes in the first Elegy: —

'O give him many thanks, he is courteous,
That in suspecting kindly warneth us.
We must not, as we us'd flout openly,
In scoffing riddles, his deformity;

Nor at his board together being sat,
With words, nor touch, scarce looks adulterate,
Nor when he swollen, and pamper'd with great fare,
Sits down, and snorts, cag'd in his basket chair,
Must we usurp his own bed any more,
Nor kiss and play in his house, as before.
Now I see many dangers; for that is
His realm, his castle, and his diocese.
But if, as envious men, which would revile
Their Prince, or coin his gold, themselves exile
Into another country, and do it there,
We play in another house, what should we fear?
There we will scorne his household policies,
His seely plots, and pensionary spies,
As the inhabitants of Thames right side
Do London's Mayor; or Germans, the Pope's pride.'

Here surely is the complete cad, if the cad of genius.
For the lady herself he had the scorn of the lettered and
the experienced for the simple: —

'Nature's lay Idiot, I taught thee to love,
And in that sophistry, Oh, thou dost prove
Too subtle: Fool, thou didst not understand
The mystic language of the eye and hand:
Nor couldst thou judge the difference of the air
Of sighs, and say, this lies, this sounds despair:
Nor by the eyes water call a malady
Desperately hot, or changing feverously.
I had not taught thee then, the Alphabet
Of flowers, how they devisefully being set
And bound up, might with speechless secrecy
Deliver errands mutely, and mutually.'

63

After a year the lover grew cold. Perhaps the lady wearied him. Perhaps he began to fear that the liaison would prejudice his career. In a temporary parting, with an emphasis on the crudity of the connection, not to be ignored if the character of the future Dean is to be understood, there is the hint — perhaps the hopeful hint — that the parting may be permanent.

'Have we not kept our guards, like spy on spy?
Had correspondence whilst the foe stood by?
Stolen (more to sweeten them) our many blisses
Of meetings, conference, embracements, kisses?
Shadow'd with negligence our most respects?
Varied our language through all dialects,
Of becks, winks, looks, and often under-boards
Spoke dialogues with our feet far from our words?
Have we prov'd all these secrets of our Art,
Yea, thy pale inwards, and thy panting heart?
And, after all this passed Purgatory
Must sad divorce make us the vulgar story?'

The liaison finished first with some regret and finally with brutal bitterness. The poet does not deny that his mistress has at least left him happy memories: —

'Time shall not lose our passages; the Spring
How fresh our love was in the beginning;
The Summer how it ripened in the ear;
And Autumn, what our golden harvests were.
The Winter, I'll not think on to spite thee,
But count it a lost season, so shall she.'

But satiety and the consequent self-hatred stirred the venom so constantly to be found in Donne. His lady is

denounced as his murderess, and he threatens that his
ghost shall haunt her guilty bed: —

'What I will say, I will not tell thee now,
Lest that preserve thee; and since my love is spent,
I had rather thou shouldst painfully repent,
Then by my threatnings rest still innocent.'

A recent writer claims that the poems from which I
have quoted show Donne as 'the first of the great seven-
teenth-century realists.' They certainly show him as a
poet of originality and brutal power. He represents
the reaction against the euphuistic sentimentality of the
Elizabethans. He is acclaimed by his admirers for his
honesty. In the years before his marriage, love to him
was entirely sensual, and he would not pretend that it
was anything else. But searching for the man's realities
in his writing, I find consistency equally unpleasant in
the jeers at a forsaken religion and in the jeers at an
abandoned mistress.

In 1597 Donne was appointed secretary to Sir Thomas
Egerton, the Lord Keeper, an eminent lawyer and a man
of sober and dignified character. Donne was then twenty-
four, young as he was, with a character affected by
cosmopolitan experience and many amatory adventures.
His five years' connection with the Lord Keeper caused a
change if not in his character, certainly in his mode of life.
The change appears to have been the result partly of the
fear of losing his patron's favour and partly of the fact
that by this time he must have spent most of the fortune
inherited from his father, mainly probably during his
continental wanderings. Doubtless, too, he was influenced
by the fate of his old patron Essex, who was tried and

executed while he was in Egerton's employ. But if, as is believed, the poem 'The Blossom' belongs to this period, he had certainly lost none of his cynical attitude to women. The last lines are: —

> 'Meet me at London, then,
> Twenty days hence, and thou shalt see
> Me fresher, and more fat, by being with men,
> Then if I had stayed still with her and thee.
> For God's sake, if you can, be you so too:
> I would give you
> There, to another friend, whom we shall find
> As glad to have my body, as my mind.'

Donne told the admiring Izaak Walton that while in the service of the Lord Keeper, he proceeded 'with humility and diffidence' in the search for religion. But there is little humility, diffidence, or care for religion in the bewildering 'The Progress of the Soul' which, written in 1601, is one of the great achievements of the poet's life. It is, indeed, a forced mocking satire, with an admittedly puerile idea, and few critics will accept De Quincey's assertion that 'massy diamonds compose the very substance of this poem on the Metempsychosis, thoughts and descriptions which have the fervent and gloomy sublimity of Ezechiel or Æschylus.' In a striking and happy phrase Sir Edmund Gosse describes the style of the poem as a 'violently varied tonality,' and in an equally happy comparison he says that Donne's revolt against the smooth sugariness of the writing of his time has had its parallel in Wagner's revolt against the similar smoothness of composers like Donizetti.

The poem which was originally called 'Metempsy-

chosis' – it may perhaps have been suggested to Donne
by a famous passage in Marlowe's Faust – has a preface
in which the poet declares that 'the Pythagorean doctrine
doth not onely carry one soule from man to man, nor man
to beast, but indifferently to plants also: and therefore
you must not grudge to finde the same soule in an Emper-
our, in a Post-horse, and in a Mucheron, since no un-
readinesse in the soule, but an indisposition in the organs
works this. And therefore though this soule could not
move when it was a Melon, yet it may remember, and
now tell mee, at what lascivious banquet it was serv'd.
And though it could not speake, when it was a spider,
yet it can remember, and now tell me, who used it for
poyson to attaine dignitie. How ever the bodies have
dull'd her other faculties, her memory hath ever been her
owne, which makes me so seriously deliver you by her
relation all her passages from her first making when shee
was that apple which Eve ate, to this time when she is she
whose life you shall finde in the end of this booke.'

She 'whose life you shall finde in the end of this booke,'
was evidently Queen Elizabeth. From Eve to Elizabeth
is a long journey, and the grandiose scheme was not
carried out. Ben Jonson, Donne's one literary friend,
said: 'The conceit of Donne's Transformation or Metempsychosis was that he sought the soule of that aple which
Eve pulled and thereafter made it the soule of a bitch,
then of a shee wolf, and so of a woman; his generall purpose was to have brought in all the bodies of the Here-
ticks from the soule of sin, and at last left in the bodie of
Calvin. Of this he never wrotte but one sheet, and now,
since he was made Doctor, repenteth highlie and seeketh
to destroy all his poems.'

The repentance is at least easy to understand. The moods of the poem are contradictory. In the fourth stanza the poet is as pessimistic and determinative as Thomas Hardy. He refers to: —

'Great Destiny the Commissary of God,
That hast mark'd out a path and period
For every thing. . . .'

But in the sixth stanza occur the magnificent lines: —

'For though through many straits, and lands I roam,
I launch at paradise, and I sail towards home;'

And one remembers the similar gleam of hope at the end of Hardy's *The Dynasts*: —

'But — a stirring thrills the air
Like to sounds of joyance there
That the rages
Of the ages
Shall be cancelled, and deliverance offered from the darts
that were,
Consciousness the Will informing, till it fashion all things
fair!'

The story of the Metempsychosis begins in the ninth stanza when the soul is in the apple of Eden, and Eve's tempting of Adam inspires the lines: —

'Man all at once was there by woman slain,
And one by one we are here slain o'er again
By them. The mother poison'd the well-head,
The daughters here corrupt us, Rivulets;

No smallness scapes, no greatness breaks their nets;
She thrusts us out, and by them we are led
Astray, from turning, to whence we are fled.
Were prisoners Judges, 'twould seem rigorous
She sinn'd, we bear; part of our pain is, thus
    To love them, whose fault to this painful love yoak'd
    us.'

From the apple the soul goes to a mandrake, then to
a sparrow, and then to a fish, and Donne writes: —

'Is any kind subject to rape like fish?
Ill unto man, they neither do, nor wish:
Fishers they kill not, nor with noise awake,
They do not hunt, nor strive to make a prey
Of beasts, nor their young sons to bear away;
Fowls they pursue not, nor do undertake
To spoil the nests industrious birds do make;
Yet them all these unkind kinds feed upon,
To kill them is an occupation,
    And laws make Feasts, and Lents for their destruction.'

It is not true, of course, that fishes 'do not hunt, nor
strive to make a prey,' but the harmlessness of the fish
had to be emphasized to prove the cruelty of nature.
Even pious fasting means death for the fish. From the
fish the soul journeys to a sea bird, to a whale, to a mouse,
to a wolf, to an ape, and at last to a woman: —

'Of every past shape, she knew treachery,
Rapine, deceit, and lust, and ills enow
To be a woman. *Themech* she is now,
    Sister and wife to *Caine*, *Caine* that first did plough.'

And there the poet finished at the first stage of the long journey which, again to quote Sir Edmund Gosse, would have taken millions of verses to conclude.

The last lines are: —

'Ther's nothing simply good, nor ill alone,
Of every quality comparison,
The only measure is, and judge, opinion.'

The poem is a magnificent failure, a curiosity rather than a treasure of literature, bitter, hard, the gibes of disappointed and unappreciated talent.

In 1601, Donne secretly married Anne More, the Lord Keeper's niece by marriage. Izaak Walton says, 'He – I dare not say unhappily – fell into such a liking as with her approbation increased into a love.' But to quote Leslie Stephen's phrase, 'A clandestine marriage with a girl of sixteen who lived in his patron's house, was a singular blunder for an ambitious young man at the outset of his career,' a blunder indeed pleasantly inconsistent with Donne's general self-seeking. As Dr. Jessop says, 'A double offence had been committed by the parties concerned. First an offence against the Canon Law in marrying a girl without the consent of her father and, secondly, a civil offence against the Common Law, it was a very serious business,' so serious indeed that it lost Donne the friendship of the Lord Keeper, aroused the fierce anger of his father-in-law and secured him a term of imprisonment in the Fleet. Donne wrote to Sir George More: —

'Sir, I acknowledge my fault to be so great, as I dare scarce offer any other prayer to you in mine own behalf than this, to believe this truth – that I neither had dishonest end nor means. But for her, whom I tender much more than my fortunes or life (else I would, I might neither joy in this life or enjoy the next), I humbly beg of you that she may not, to her danger, feel the terror of your sudden anger.

'I know this letter shall find you full of passion; but I know no passion can alter your reason and wisdom, to which I adventure to commend these particulars; – that it is irremediably done; that if you incense my lord, you destroy her and me; that it is easy to give us happiness, and that my endeavours and industry, if it please you to prosper them, may soon make me somewhat worthier of her.

'If any take the advantage of your displeasure against me, and fill you with ill thoughts of me, my comfort is that you know that faith and thanks are due to them only that speak when their informations might do good, which now it cannot work towards any party. For my excuse I can say nothing, except I knew what were said to you.

'Sir, I have truly told you this matter, and I humbly beseech you so to deal in it as the persuasions of Nature, Reason, Wisdom, and Christianity shall inform you; and to accept the vows of one whom you may now raise or scatter – which are, that as my love is directed unchangeably upon her, so all my labours shall concur to her contentment, and to show my humble obedience to yourself.

'Yours in all duty and humbleness,'

But More was furiously angry and insisted on punishment, and on February 10, 1603, Donne was imprisoned in the Fleet. He again wrote to his father-in-law: –

'Almighty God, whom I call to witness that all my grief is that I have in this manner offended you and Him, direct you to believe that which out of an humble and afflicted heart I now write to you. And since we have no means to move God, when He will not hear our prayers, to hear them, but by praying, I humbly beseech you to allow by His gracious example my penitence so good entertainment, as it may have a belief and a pity.

'Of nothing in this one fault that I hear said to me can I disculp myself, but of the contemptuous and despiteful purpose towards you, which I hear is surmised against me. But for my dutiful regard to my late Lady, for my religion, and for my life, I refer myself to them that may have observed them. I humbly beseech you to take off these weights, and to put my fault into the balance alone, as it was done without the addition of these ill reports, and though then it will be too heavy for me, yet then it will less grieve you to pardon it.

'How little and how short the comfort and pleasure of destroying is, I know your wisdom and religion informs you. And though perchance you intend not utter destruction, yet the way through which I fall towards it is so headlong, that, being thus pushed, I shall soon be at bottom, for it pleaseth God, from whom I acknowledge the punishment to be just, to accompany my other ills with so much sickness as I have no refuge but that of mercy, which I beg of Him, my Lord, and you, which I hope you will not repent to have afforded me, since all my endeavours and the whole course of my life shall be bent to make myself worthy of your favour and her love, whose peace of conscience and quiet I know must be much wounded and violenced if your displeasure sever us.'

An appeal even more exaggerated in its humility to the Lord Keeper secured his release from prison with the order that he should be confined in his chamber in the Strand, and this inspired a third letter to Sir George More, almost nauseous in its grovelling flattery. He wrote: —

'Sir, From you, to whom next to God I shall owe my health, by enjoying your mediation this mild change of imprisonment, I desire to derive all my good fortune and content in this world; and therefore, with my most unfeigned thanks, present to you my humble petition that you would be pleased to hope that, as that fault which was laid to me of having deceived some gentlewomen before, and that of loving a corrupt religion, are vanished and smoked away (as I assure myself, out of their weakness they are), and that as the devil in the article of our death takes the advantage of our weakness and fear to aggravate our sins or our conscience, so some uncharitable malice hath presented my debts double at least.

'How many of the imputations laid upon me would fall off, if I might shake and purge myself in your presence! But if that were done, of this offence committed to you I cannot acquit myself, of which yet I hope that God (to Whom for that I heartily direct many prayers) will inform you to make that use, that as of evil manners good laws grow, so out of disobedience and boldness you will take occasion to show mercy and tenderness. And when it shall please God to soften your heart so much towards us as to pardon us, I beseech you also to undertake that charitable office of being my mediator to my Lord, whom as upon your just complaint you found full of justice, I

doubt not but you shall also find full of mercy, for so is
the Almighty pattern of Justice and Mercy equally full
of both.

'My conscience, and such affection as in my conscience
becomes an honest man, emboldeneth me to make one
request more, which is, that by some kind and comfortable message you would be pleased to give some ease of
the afflictions which I know your daughter in her mind
suffers, and that (if it be not against your other purposes)
I may with your leave write to her, for without your leave
I will never attempt anything concerning her. God so
have mercy upon me, as I am unchangeably resolved to
bend all my courses to make me fit for her, which if God
and my Lord and you be pleased to strengthen, I hope
neither my debts, which I can easily order, nor anything
else shall interrupt. Almighty God keep you in His
favour, and restore me to His and yours.'

The denial that he has been guilty of loving a 'corrupt
religion' is in the circumstances particularly nauseous.
There is every reason to believe that Donne was genuinely in love with Anne More, and his marriage marks
the beginning of a new development in his character.
But he must certainly have known her when he wrote
'The Progress of the Soul,' and there is little evidence in
it of that softening power of love on which his eulogists
insist. After his marriage, there is an obvious change of
mood. In the early days when he was separated from his
wife, he wrote a poem called 'The Canonization,' which
has striking lyrical beauty: —

'For Godsake hold your tongue, and let me love,
    Or chide my palsy, or my gout,

74

My five gray hairs, or ruin'd fortune flout,
  With wealth your state, your mind with Arts improve,
Take you a course, get you a place,
Observe his honour, or his grace,
Or the Kings reall, or his stamped face
Contemplate, what you will, approve,
So you will let me love.'

In poem after poem his love for his wife finds its
expression. For example: —

  'I scarce believe my love to be so pure
      As I had thought it was,
      Because it doth endure
  Vicissitude, and season, as the grass;
  Methinks I lied all winter, when I swore
  My love was infinite, if spring make it more.'

For three or four years after his marriage, Donne
lived with his wife's relations and then he moved to a
house in Mitcham, a damp and uncomfortable dwelling
where he proceeded to beget a considerable number of
rickety children.   In 1605 and 1606 he was busy as-
sisting Thomas Morton in his pamphlet war with the
Jesuits. The new convert was eager to demonstrate his
zeal.

While, too, he was living at Mitcham, he made a
journey to Italy, and his wife, still a mere girl, proposed
to go with him as a page. The jesting proposal inspired
some really delightful lines: —

  'By our first strange and fatal interview,
  By all desires which thereof did ensue,
  By our long starving hopes, by that remorse
  Which my words' masculine persuasive force

75

Begot in thee, and by the memory
Of hurts, which spies and rivals threaten'd me,
I calmly beg. But by thy father's wrath,
By all pains, which want and divorcement hath,
I conjure thee, and all the oaths which I
And thou have sworn to seal joint constancy,
Here I unswear, and overswear them thus;
Thou shalt not love by ways so dangerous.
Temper, O fair love, love's impetuous rage;
Be my true mistress still, not my feign'd page.
I'll go, and, by thy kind leave, leave behind
Thee, only worthy to nurse in my mind
Thirst to come back; O! if thou die before,
My soul from other lands to thee shall soar.
Thy else-almighty beauty cannot move
Rage from the seas, nor thy love teach them love.'

His financial position had now become extremely uncomfortable. He had spent most of his patrimony long
before his marriage, and although his wife's connections
were rich, supplies were intermittent. He had no established position. His family was increasing and he was
eager to find some well-paid employment. It was suggested to him that this would most easily be found if he
were to take Holy Orders, and to this he was urged both
by his patron, Morton, and by King James. But it is to
Donne's credit that at first he refused. Izaak Walton
records that he said to Morton: —

'I dare make so dear a friend as you are my confessor:
some irregularities of my life have been so visible to some
men, that though I have, I thank God, made my peace
with Him by penitential resolution against them and

76

by the assistance of His grace, banished them my affections: yet this, which God knows to be so, is not so visible to men, as to free me from their censures, and, it may be, that sacred calling from a dishonour. And besides, whereas it is determined by the best of casuists that God's glory should be the first end, and a maintenance the second motive to embrace that calling; and though each man may propose to himself both together; yet the first may not be put last without a violation of conscience, which He that searches the heart will judge. And truly my present condition is such, that if I ask my own conscience, whether it be reconcilable to that rule, it is at this time so perplexed about it, that I can neither give myself nor you an answer. You know, sir, who says, Happy is that man whose conscience doth not accuse him for that thing which he does. To these, I might add other reasons that dissuade me; but I crave your favour that I may forbear to express them, and thankfully decline your offer.'

His father-in-law, quite naturally, refused to provide for him and his family, and in the miserable little house at Mitcham the poet spent wearing and unhappy years. 'I write from the fireside in my parlour,' he said in one of his letters, 'and in the noise of three gamesome children and by the side of her whom, because I have transplanted into such a wretched fortune, I must labour to disguise that from her by all such honest devices as giving her my company and discourse.' This letter suggests that there must have been many gloomy evenings at Mitcham for poor Mrs. Donne.

The letters of Donne at this time were persistently

importunate. Sometimes he flew high, as in asking to be British Ambassador to the Republic of Venice. Generally he was more humble in his requests. At last, almost in despair, he contemplated suicide and wrote a long dissertation proving that to kill oneself can hardly be regarded as a deadly sin. He says: —

'Since I may without flying, or eating, when I have means, attend an executioner, or famine; since I may offer my life, even for another's temporal good; since I must do it for his spiritual; since I may give another my board (plank) in a shipwreck, and so drown; since I may hasten my arrival to heaven by consuming penances, — it is a wayward and unnoble stubbornness in argument to say still, I must not kill myself, but I may let myself die; since, of affirmations and denials, of omissions and committings, of enjoining and prohibitory commands, ever the one implies and enwraps the other. And if the matter shall be resolved and governed only by an outward act, and ever by that; if I forbear to swim (when thrown into) a river, and so perish, because there is no act, I shall not be guilty; and yet I shall be guilty if I discharge a pistol upon myself, which I know not to be charged, nor intended harm, because there is an act.'

His interest in religion grew greater — it may have been a relaxation in the prevailing dull dampness — and he was drawn more and more to the middle way, beloved of the English Church. He would not, he said, immure religion 'in a Rome or a Wittenberg or a Geneva,' and he added: —

'You know I never fettered nor imprisoned the word Religion, not straightening it friarly, *ad Religiones facti-*

tias (as the Romans call well their orders of Religion), nor immuring it in a Rome, or a Wittenberg, or a Geneva; they are all virtual beams of one Sun, wheresoever they find clay hearts, they harden them and moulder them into dust; and they entender and mollify waxen. They are not so contrary as the North and South Poles, and that (?) they are co-natural pieces of one circle. Religion is Christianity, which being too spiritual to be seen by us, doth therefore take an apparent body of good life and works, so salvation requires an honest Christian.'

Donne was genuinely in love with his wife and had done with wantonness. He had made the journey from polygamy to monogamy, which, it is said, most men make, though perhaps quite as many travel in the other way. Family cares and Mitcham tended to induce serious-mindedness. Repentance encouraged casuistry in a very subtle mind and a professional connection with religious controversy had its effect in the sententiousness of his advice to his friend, Sir Henry Goodyear: —

'However, keep the lively taste you hold
 Of God, love him as now, but fear him more,
And in your afternoons think what you told
 And promis'd him, at morning prayer before.'

This period of his life was a time of great activity, Donne using all his talents to obtain the favour of the court and consequent employment. His clever, partisan *Pseudo-Martyr* was written, so Walton says, in six weeks and at the suggestion of King James. It is an attack on the Roman Catholic recusants who preferred to suffer rather than to take the oath of allegiance to the

King as head of the Church as well as of the State. The descendant of a family of martyrs denied the dignity of martyrdom to men whom he declared, 'urge, provoke and importune affliction,' and he advised that 'just love of your own safety' which martyrs in all ages have invariably disregarded.

He declared that it had taken some time for him to become emancipated from the influence of Rome 'although I apprehended well enough that this irresolution not only retarded my fortune, but also bred some scandal.' Forgetting the sufferings of his uncles, he suggested that the recusants were merely pseudo-martyrs, and that if they suffered death for their obstinacy, they were guilty of suicide. He proceeds to examine the doctrine of Purgatory and concludes: 'Purgatory seems to me to be the Mythologie of the Roman Church and a morall application of pious and useful fables.' If Donne were living now he would presumably be considerably startled by the acceptance by the Bishops of the English Church of the doctrine of purgatorial progress implied in the New Prayer Book: 'O Almighty God, the God of the spirits of all flesh, multiply we beseech thee to those who rest in Jesus the manifold blessing of thy love that the good work which thou didst begin in them may be perfected unto the day of Jesus Christ.'

Ignatius His Conclaves is a bitter satirical attack on the Jesuits, and particularly on St. Ignatius who, in the writer's dream, is the chief favourite of Lucifer in Hell. The founder of the Society of Jesus is politely described as 'this French-Spanish mongrel,' and the ex-Roman Catholic denounces Rome and its Popes with all the bitterness common to a pervert. In this satire, Donne, who was keenly interested in the scientific discoveries of the age, shows himself familiar with the achievements of Kepler and Galileo.

If *The Pseudo-Martyr* and *Ignatius His Conclaves* were calculated to secure the official employment for which Donne sought so long in vain, another work of his at this time was equally calculated to offend. And with his characteristic subtleness he forbade its publication during his lifetime. This is *Biathanatos*, the defence of suicide.

It is not perhaps surprising that Donne like other men with large families and small means should have thought of suicide as a way out of his troubles, but I do not believe that he ever seriously considered his own self-destruction, and *Biathanatos* is merely ingenious special pleading. Following the argument of *The Pseudo-Martyr* he suggests that martyrdom itself is suicide. To kill oneself is at least to escape from the defilements of this earthly life: —

'When he withdraws and purges (his body) from all corruptions (by killing himself), he delivers it from all the inquinations and venom and malign machinations of his and God's adversaries, and prepares it by God's insinuation and concurrence to that glory, which, without death, cannot be attained.'

The letters written during these years clearly suggest the step which common decency had hitherto compelled him to postpone. Ever since his marriage he had been living more or less uncomfortably at other people's expense. He was now nearly forty. He had failed in all his applications for secular employment, and he was now compelled to admit, in Dr. Jessop's words, 'if not Church preferment, then none at all.'

It is curious that he began to write definitely religious poetry at the time when he was becoming more and more convinced that only in the Church could he find a tolerable livelihood. In 1608, he wrote 'The Litany,' the first of his religious poems, characterized far more by intellectual pedantry than by religious fervour. In an address to Our Lady, Donne shows that while he was no longer a Roman Catholic, he was not – I do not think, by the way, that he ever was – a violent Protestant, though there is of course nothing in his veneration of Our Lady incompatible with the doctrines of the English Church: –

'For that fair blessed Mother-maid
Whose flesh redeem'd us; That she-Cherubim,
   Which unlock'd Paradise, and made
One claim for innocence, and disseiz'd sin,
   Whose womb was a strange heav'n for there
   God cloth'd himself, and grew,
Our zealous thanks we pour. As her deeds were
   Our helps, so are her prayers; nor can she sue
   In vain, who had such titles unto you.'

In 'The Cross,' another religious poem written at Mitcham, he writes: –

'Who can blot out the Cross, which th' instrument
Of God, dew'd on me in the Sacrament?
Who can deny me power, and liberty
To stretch mine arms, and mine own Cross to be?
Swim, and at every stroke, thou art thy Cross;
The Mast and yard make one, where seas do toss;

Look down, thou spiest out Crosses in small things;
Look up, thou seest birds rais'd on crossed wings;
All the Globe's frame, and spheres, is nothing else
But the Meridians crossing Parallels.'

How trivial and involved and essentially un-Christian it is! How obvious is the effort of the writer, with no real religious sense, to learn the use of sacred imagery.

In 1610, Donne earned the favour of Sir Robert Drury and incidentally 'a useful apartment' in that wealthy knight's house in Drury Lane, by writing a hyperbolic eulogy of his daughter Elizabeth, who died in her youth and whom Donne had never seen. It is characterized by what is for Donne a rare smoothness and simplicity. He writes: —

'One, whose clear body was so pure and thin,
Because it need disguise no thought within.
'Twas but a through-light scarf, her mind t'enroll;
Or exhalation breath'd out from her Soul.
One, whom all men who durst no more, admir'd:
And whom, who ere had worth enough, desir'd;
As when a Temple's built, Saints emulate
To which of them, it shall be consecrate.'

By the way of rent for the useful apartment in Drury Lane, Donne wrote a second poem, 'An Anatomy of the World,' on the first anniversary of Elizabeth's death, and another, 'The Progress of the Soul,' on the second anniversary. No poet was ever so eager to make friends for himself of mammon. 'The Anatomy of the World' is indecent in its fulsomeness and disgusted Donne's friends, Ben Jonson declaring that it was 'profane and full of blasphemies.' It is resplendently insincere, the blatant buying the favour of a rich man. Yet it contains some fine passages, the third of these three lines, for example: —

> 'Doth not a Teneriffe, or higher Hill
> Rise so high like a Rock, that one might think
> The floating Moon would shipwreck there, and sink?

Other great ladies, whose friendship was of value, were seriously annoyed by Donne's rhapsodizing over Elizabeth Drury, and he realized that he had overdone his flattery and overpaid his rent. He wrote to the Countess of Bradford: —

> 'First I confess I have to others lent
>   Your stock, and over prodigally spent
> Your treasure, for since I had never known
>   Virtue or beauty, but as they are grown
> In you, I should not think or say they shine,
>   (So as I have) in any other Mine.'

Sir Robert Drury was not a niggardly paymaster. In 1612 he took Donne on a foreign tour. His wife was ill. She had had her eighth child, which died at birth, and she was unwilling to be left alone, probably with a very thin purse. To appease her, Donne wrote 'Sweetest Love, I Do Not Go,' to me the most delightful of his poems: —

> 'Sweetest love, I do not go
>   For weariness of thee,
> Nor in hope the world can show
>   A fitter love for me,

But since that I
At the last must part, 'tis best,
Thus to use myself in jest
By feigned deaths to die.

'Yesternight the sun went hence,
And yet is here to-day;
He hath no desire nor sense,
Nor half so short a way;
Then fear not me,
But believe that I shall make
Speedier journeys, since I take
More wings and spurs than he.

'O how feeble is man's power
That if good fortune fall,
Cannot add another hour,
Nor a lost hour recall;
But come bad chance,
And we join to it our strength,
And we teach it art and length,
Itself o'er us to advance.

'When thou sigh'st, thou sigh'st not wind,
But sigh'st my soul away;
When thou weep'st, unkindly kind,
My life's blood doth decay.
It cannot be
That thou lov'st me as thou say'st,
If in thine my life thou waste,
That art the best of me.

'Let not thy divining heart
  Forethink me any ill;
Destiny may take thy part,
  And may thy fears fulfil.
    But think that wc
Are but turn'd aside to sleep;
They who one another keep
  Alive, ne'er parted be.'

Walton says that at this time, and again to please the deserted wife, Donne also wrote the Valediction forbidding Mourning, which concludes: —

'Our two souls therefore, which are one,
  Though I must go, endure not yet
A breach, but an expansion,
  Like gold to every thinness beat.

'If they be two, they are two so
  As stiff twin compasses are two,
Thy soul the fixed foot, makes no show
  To move, but doth, if the other do.

'And though it in the centre sit,
  Yet when the other far doth roam,
It leans, and hearkens after it,
  And grows erect, as that comes home.

'Such wilt thou be to me, who must
  Like th' other foot, obliquely run;
Thy firmness makes my circle just,
  And makes me end, where I begun.'

Shortly after Donne's return from the Continent the Princess Elizabeth, from whom the present British royal

family is descended, was married to the Elector Palatine
on St. Valentine's Day, and Donne, eager Court poet in
search of better employment, wrote her marriage song.
It opens: —

'Hail, Bishop Valentine, whose day this is;
 All the air is thy diocese.
 And all the chirping choristers
And other birds are thy parishioners;
 Thou marriest every year
The lyric lark, and the grave whispering dove,
The sparrow that neglects his life for love,
The household bird with the red stomacher;
 Thou mak'st the blackbird speed as soon
As doth the goldfinch or the halcyon;
The husband-cock looks out, and straight is sped,
And meets his wife, who brings her feather-bed;
This day more cheerfully than ever shine;
This day, which might inflame thyself, old Valentine.'

In these years, and just before his ordination, occurred
the most offensive incident in a perplexing career. The
story of Rochester and the Countess of Essex is the foulest
incident in a reign, the general foulness of which good
Protestant historians ingeniously ignore. Rochester was a
blackguard. The woman was a ruthless and reckless
wanton. Yet to Rochester, Donne, who can hardly have
been ignorant of his character, wrote a series of disgust-
ingly fulsome letters, asking his aid in securing ordination.
Although Donne was not a lawyer, he had considerable
legal knowledge which must have been of immense use
to his patron. It has been urged that Donne had no
direct part in the trial and that he has been confused

with Sir Daniel Donne, the Dean of Arches. But all the excuses of apologetic biographers cannot disprove the charge that in his relations with Rochester, Donne behaved with extreme baseness, and it is not without some satisfaction that one records that the promised reward was never forthcoming.

The year 1614 found Donne hopelessly depressed. He was ill, his children were dying one after the other, he had sold his soul for nothing. Donne's character and state of mind at this particular time was demonstrated in a letter that he wrote to Rochester: —

'It is now somewhat more than a year since I took the boldness to make my purpose of professing divinity known to your Lordship, as to a person whom God had made so great an instrument of His providence in this kingdom, as that nothing in it should be done without your knowledge, your Lordship exercised upon me then many of your virtues, for besides, that by your bounty I have lived ever since, it hath been through your Lordship's advice and inspiration of new hopes into me that I have lived cheerfully. By this time, perchance, your Lordship may have discerned that the malignity of my ill-fortune may infect your good, and that by some impressions in your Lordship I may be incapable of the favours which your Lordship had purposed to me. I had rather perish than be such a rub in your fortune, or that through me your history should have one example of having missed what you desired; I humbly therefore beg of your Lordship that after you shall have been pleased to admit into your memory that I am now a year older, broken with some sickness, and in the same degree of honesty as I was, your Lordship will afford me one commandment, and bid me either hope for this business in your Lordship's hand, or else pursue my first purpose or abandon all; for as I cannot live without your favour, so I cannot die without your leave; because even by dying I should steal from you one who is by his own devotions and your purchase your Lordship's most humble and thankful servant.'

Rochester and the Countess of Essex were married in the winter of 1613, and Donne did not hesitate to write an Epithalamium on the wedding of the 'blest pair of swans,' which is as felicitous in phrasing as it is disgraceful in intention. The following is a description of the bride and bridegroom going to the chapel: –

'Now from your easts you issue forth, and we, –
   As men, which thro' a cypress see
   The rising sun, do think it two,
So, as you go to church, – do think of you;
    But that veil being gone,
By the church-rites you are from henceforth one.

'The church triumphant made this match before,
And now the militant doth strive no more.
Then, reverend Priest, who God's recorder art,
Do, from His dictates, to these two impart
All blessings which are seen or thought, by angel's
   eye or heart.'

Never were crime and debauchery more thoroughly tawned upon by genius! To suggest that the Church triumphant had anything to do with such a marriage is the crudest of blasphemies.

In 1614 Donne made another effort to court the favour of the Crown by writing a bitter comment on Sir Walter Raleigh's *History of the World*, written while its author was in the Tower and soon to be taken to the execution block. As Bacon deserted Essex, so Donne maligned his old leader, Raleigh. And again a mean service was rendered without reward. 'No man attends Court fortunes with more impatience than I do,' he said. No man, indeed, ever asked for favours more persistently or more unsuccessfully. The King seems to have made up his mind that Donne's talents fitted him for the Church and for nothing else, and at long last he was ordained on the feast of the Conversion of St. Paul, 1615, in St. Paul's Cathedral. He was, as it has been truly said, 'starved into submission to the King's will.' He served for a short time as a curate in Paddington, and though he had obeyed the royal command, there was a considerable delay in his preferment. He was still troubled by his debts and he went on imploring other people's aid with the enthusiasm of a modern begging-letter writer. New children, too, continued to arrive at regular intervals.

In 1615 he received the degree of Doctor of Divinity from the University of Cambridge and preached his first sermon before the King at Whitehall. Of his eloquence there can be no question. Izaak Walton rhapsodized over his sermon, describing the preacher as 'carrying some, as St. Paul was, to heaven in holy raptures, and enticing others by a sacred art and courtship to amend their lives.'

In 1616 Donne was presented to a small living in Huntingdonshire and soon afterwards he became rector

of Sevenoaks. He retained both livings for years and
never visited either parish. Dr. Jessop endeavours to
defend the absentee parson of the seventeenth century,
but it is interesting to note that the system properly
denounced by the reformers continued long after the
Reformation. In the autumn of the same year Donne
was elected Divinity Reader to the benchers at Lincoln's Inn, where he had entered as a student years
before. This appointment brought his money anxieties
to an end. He had not taken Holy Orders in vain!

His wife died in 1617, having borne twelve children,
of whom five were dead. 'It was the loss of his wife,'
says Sir Edmund Gosse, 'which brought about the final
process of sanctification and illumination.' That may be,
though it might be more cynically suggested that Donne
got religion when he got perferment. Sir Edmund
Gosse says: 'In every word of that fine writing by or
about Donne from January, 1615, to the winter of 1617,
I discover a decency, but no ardour; a conventional piety,
but no holy zeal; no experience of spiritual joy; no humility before God. After the death of his wife I find all
these gifts in their full fruition. I am therefore forced
to conclude that in the winter of 1617 Donne passed
through a crisis of what is called "conversion"; that he
became sanctified and illuminated in a sense in which he
had not been sanctified before.' Izaak Walton says:
'Now to the English Church it meant a second St.
Austin; for I think none was so like him before his
conversion, none so like St. Ambrose after it, and if his
youth had the infirmities of the one, his age had the
excellencies of the other.' But Sir Edmund Gosse is
clearly right. The beginning of his religious life dates

from the death of his wife and certainly not from the time of his ordination.

It is more often the passionate than the cold who at last find refuge and satisfaction in the love of God. It was natural and consistent for Louise de la Vallière to fly from Versailles to a convent cell. It was equally natural and consistent that Donne's passion and ambition should be converted into, I quote Mr. Charles Gardner, 'a single burning desire to know God and to live for His glory.' He had never escaped from the influence of the mystics whom he had learned to know at Oxford. It was, as Mr. Gardner has said in his interesting book *In Defence of the Faith*, 'the spiritual passion of St. John of the Cross and St. Theresa that had attracted him,' and in his later years he had something of their realization of mystical union with God and of the horror of banishment from His presence. 'What Tophet is not Paradise,' he said in one of his sermons, 'what brimstone is not amber, what gnashing is not comfort, what gnawing of the worm is not a tickling, what torment is not a marriage bed to this damnation, to be secluded eternally, eternally, eternally, from the sight of God.'

In 1617 Donne's religious poetry for the first time rang true. 'The Holy Sonnets' and the seven sonnets called 'La Corona' were both probably written in that year, and it is noticeable that in his new mood, Donne no longer despises the established metrical forms. The poet sorrows for his sins. His guilt is worse than that of the Jews: —

'They kill'd once an inglorious man, but I
Crucify him daily, being now glorified.'

He yearns for God, but his vision, deceived by the new learning, is God's enemy: —

> 'Take me to you, imprison me, for I
> Except you enthrall me, never shall be free,
> Nor ever chaste, except you ravish me.'

But the priest, not yet a Dean, is still a doubter. He cannot even decide which is the true Church. In the eighteenth of the 'Holy Sonnets' he says: —

'Show me, dear Christ, thy spouse, so bright and clear,
What! is it She, which on the other shore
Goes richly painted? or which rob'd and tore
Laments and mourns in Germany and here?
Sleeps she a thousand, then peeps up one year?
Is she self truth and errs, now new, now outworn?
Doth she, and did she, and shall she evermore
On one, on seven, or on no hill appear?
Dwells she with us, or like adventuring knights
First travail we to seek and then make Love?
Betray, kind husband, thy spouse to our sights
And let mine amorous soul court thy mild Dove,
Who is most true, and pleasing to thee, then
When she is embrac'd and open to most men.'

There is deep and obviously religious feeling in the poem 'Hymn to Christ' written in 1619: —

> 'In what torn ship soever I embark,
> That ship shall be the emblem of Thy ark;
> What sea soever swallow me, that flood
> Shall be to me an emblem of Thy blood;

Though Thou with clouds of anger do disguise
Thy face, yet through that mask I know those eyes
Which, tho' they turn away sometimes, yet never will
    despise.

  'I sacrifice this island unto Thee,
    And all whom I love there, and who love me;
    When I have put our seas 'twixt them and me,
    Put Thou Thy seas betwixt my sins and Thee.
    As the tree's sap doth seek the root below
    In winter, in my winter now I go
Where none but the Eternal Root of true love, I may
    know.

  'Nor Thou, nor Thy religion dost control
    The amorousness of an harmonious soul;
    But Thou would have that love Thyself; as Thou
    Art jealous, Lord, so I am jealous now;
    Thou lov'st not, till from loving more, Thou free
    My soul; whoever gives, takes liberty;
Oh! if Thou car'st not whom I love, alas! Thou lov'st
    not me.

  'Seal then this bill of my divorce to all
    On whom those fainter beams of love did fall;
    Marry those loves, which in youth scattered be
    On fame, wit, hopes – false mistresses – to Thee.
    Churches are best for prayer that have least light;
    To see God only, I go out of sight;
And, to scape stormy days, I choose an everlasting
    night.'

In 1621 Donne was appointed Dean of St. Paul's.
Walton has told the story of his appointment.

94

'The king sent to Dr. Donne, and appointed him to attend him at dinner the next day. When his Majesty was sat down, before he had any meat, he said after his pleasant manner, "Dr. Donne, I have invited you to dinner, and, though you sit not down with me, yet I will carve to you of a dish which I know you love well; for knowing you love London, I do therefore make you Dean of St. Paul's; and when I have dined, then do you take your beloved dish home to your. study, say grace there to yourself, and much good may it do you." '

Following in the footsteps of Colet, Donne's sermons at the cathedral were practical and homely, though he was eager to show his gratitude for the royal favour with sermons attacking the Puritans. In 1623 Donne was very ill, and during his convalescence he wrote a singularly beautiful hymn which Izaak Walton relates was 'set to a most grave and solemn tune and often sung to the organ by the choristers of St. Paul's church': —

'Wilt Thou forgive that sin where I begun,
    Which was my sin, though it were done before?
Wilt Thou forgive that sin through which I run,
    And do run still, though still I do deplore?
When Thou hast done, Thou hast not done,
        For I have more.

'Wilt Thou forgive that sin, which I have won
    Others to sin, and made my sin their door?
Wilt Thou forgive that sin which I did shun
    A year or two, but wallow'd in a score?
When Thou hast done, Thou hast not done,
        For I have more.

'I have a sin of fear, that when I've spun
  My last thread, I shall perish on the shore;
But swear by Thyself, that at my death Thy Son
  Shall shine as He shines now, and heretofore;
And having done that, Thou hast done,
      I fear no more.'

In 1624 Donne was chosen Prolocutor of the Lower House of Convocation and added to his preferments the vicarage of St. Dunstan's in the West. Izaak Walton lived almost next door to the church. It was suggested that he should resign the other benefices that he held, but he obstinately refused, and although his income was now considerable, he continued to grumble at its paucity.

To 1624 belongs the poem 'A Hymn to God the Father,' written in his convalescence, very human in its sorrow at the repetition of sins already often committed.

James I died on March 27, 1625, and Donne was ordered to preach before King Charles on April 2, receiving on the following day the royal commendation. During the plague of 1626, Donne stayed at Chelsea at the house of Lord Danvers, who was an old friend of his, and it was at Chelsea that he met George Herbert, a kinsman of his hostess, and wrote in thanks for her kindness the beautiful poem 'Autumnal.' Herbert had been ambitious for a politicial career, but in 1625 'God inclined him to put on a resolution to serve at His altar,' and he began eight years of holy living and the writing of poems which, in Andrew Lang's phrase, have become 'dear to many holy and humble men at heart.' Donne never appears to have met either Crawshaw or Vaughan.

As Dean of St. Paul's, Donne took particular pains to

acquire the favour of the City Fathers. By his orders the aldermen were given seats in the choir of the cathedral, in the stalls properly reserved for the clergy, and no doubt this step had a second importance in proving the Dean's essential Protestantism.

Donne died on March 31, 1631. Walton says of his last days: —

'The latter part of his life may be said to have been a continued study; for as he usually preached once a week, if not oftener, so after his sermon he never gave his eyes rest till he had chosen out a new text, and that night cast his sermon into a form, and his text into divisions; and the next day betook himself to consult the Fathers and so commit his meditations to his memory, which was excellent. But upon Saturday he usually gave himself and his mind a rest from the weary burden of the week's meditations, and usually spent that day in visitation of friends, or some other diversions of his thoughts, and would say that he gave both his body and mind that refreshment that he might be enabled to do the work of the day following, not faintly, but with courage and cheerfulness.'

Donne's last sermon was preached on February 12, and eight days before his death he wrote his last poem: —

'Since I am coming to that holy room,
   Where, with Thy Choir of Saints for evermore
I shall be made Thy music, as I come
   I tune my instrument here at the door,
   And, what I must do then, think here before.

'Whilst my physicians by their love are grown
  Cosmographers, and I their map, who lie
Flat on this bed, that by them may be shown
  That this is my south-west discovery,
  Per fretum febris, by those straits to die.

'I joy, that in these straits I see my west;
  For, though those currents yield return to none,
What shall my west hurt me. As west and east
  In all flat maps – and I am one – are one,
  So death doth touch the resurrection.

'Is the Pacific sea my home. Or are
  The eastern riches? Is Jerusalem?
Anyan, and Magellan, and Gibraltar?
  All straits, and none but straits, are ways to them
  Whether where Japhet dwelt, or Cham, or Shem.

'We think that Paradise and Calvary,
  Christ's cross and Adam's tree, stood in one place;
Look, Lord, and find both Adams met in me;
  As the first Adam's sweat surrounds my face,
  May the last Adam's blood my soul embrace.

'So, in His purple wrapp'd, receive me, Lord;
  By these His Thorns, give me His other crown;
And as to others' souls I preach'd Thy word,
  Be this my text, my sermon to mine own,
  "Therefore that He may raise, the Lord throws
    down." '

He was buried in St. Paul's Cathedral, where his
memory is perpetuated by a memorial executed according to orders given by himself just before his death.

I quote, at length, Izaak Walton's admirable description
of the Dean's last days: –

'The Sunday following he appointed his servants that, if there were any business yet undone that concerned him or themselves, it should be prepared against Saturday next, for after that day he would not mix his thoughts with anything that concerned this world, nor ever did; but as Job, so he "waited for the appointed day of his dissolution."

'And now he was so happy as to have nothing to do but to die, to do which he stood in need of no longer time; for he had studied it long, and to so happy a perfection, that in a former sickness he called God to witness (in his *Book of Devotions* written then), "He was that minute ready to deliver his soul into His hands, if that minute God would determine his dissolution." In that sickness he begged of God the constancy to be preserved in that estate for ever; and his patient expectation to have his immortal soul disrobed from her garment of mortality, makes me confident that he now had a modest assurance that his prayers were then heard, and his petition granted. He lay fifteen days earnestly expecting his hourly change; and in the last hour of his last day, as his body melted away, and vapoured into spirit, his soul having, I verily believe, some revelation of the beatifical vision, he said, "I were miserable if I might not die": and after those words, closed many periods of his faint breath by saying often, "Thy kingdom come, Thy will be done." His speech, which had long been his ready and faithful servant, left him not till the last minute of his life, and then forsook him, not to serve another master — for who speaks like him, — but died before him; for that it was then become useless to him, that now conversed with God on earth as angels are said to do in heaven, only by thoughts and looks. Being speechless, and seeing heaven by that illumination by which he saw it, he did, as St. Stephen, "look steadfastly into it, till he saw the Son of Man standing at the right hand of God His Father," and being satisfied with this blessed sight, as his soul ascended and his last breath departed from him, he closed his own eyes, and then disposed his. hands and body into such a posture as required not the least alteration by those that came to shroud him.

'He was buried in that place of St. Paul's Church which he had appointed for that use some years before his death, and by which he passed daily to pay his public devotions to Almighty God, who was then served twice a day by a public form of prayer and praise in that place; but he was not buried privately, though he desired it, for, beside an unnumbered number of others, many persons of nobility and of eminence for learning, who did love and honour him in his life, did show it at his death, by a voluntary and sad attendance of his body to the grave, where nothing was so remarkable as a public sorrow.

'To which place of his burial some mournful friends repaired, and, as Alexander the Great did to the grave of the famous Achilles, so they strewed his with an abundance of curious and costly flowers, which course they, who were never yet known, continued morning and evening for many days, not ceasing till the stones that were taken up in that church to give his body admission into the cold earth – now his bed of rest – were again by the mason's art so levelled and firmed as they had been formerly, and his place of burial undistinguishable to common view.

'The next day after his burial some unknown friend, some one of the many lovers and admirers of his virtue and learning, writ this epitaph with a coal on the wall over his grave : —

> "Reader! I am to let thee know,
> Donne's body only lies below;
> For, could the grave his soul comprise,
> Earth would be richer than the skies!"

'Nor was this all the honour done to his reverend ashes; for, as there be some persons that will not receive a reward for that for which God accounts Himself a debtor, persons that dare trust God with their charity, and without a witness, so there was by some grateful unknown friend that thought Dr. Donne's memory ought to be perpetuated, a hundred marks sent to his faithful friends and executors (Dr. King and Dr. Montfort), towards the making of his monument. It was not for many years known by whom; but, after the death of Dr. Fox, it was known that it was he that sent it, and he lived to see as lively a representation of his dead friend as marble can express; a statue indeed so like Dr. Donne, that — as his friend Sir Henry Wotton hath expressed himself — "It seems to breathe faintly, and posterity shall look upon it as a kind of artificial miracle."

'He was of stature moderately tall, of a straight and equally proportioned body, to which all his words and actions gave an unexpressible addition of comeliness.

'The melancholy and pleasant humour were in him so contempered that each gave advantage to the other, and made his company one of the delights of mankind.

'His fancy was unimitably high, equalled only by his

great wit, both being made useful by a commanding judgment.'

Donne was a handsome man of middle height, notable for his elegance of manner. He was whimsical, passionate and soft-hearted, subject to fits of melancholy and easily depressed. Sir Edmund Gosse finds him 'the most undulating, the most diverse of human beings,' and hints at the mystery of his character. But to me there is little mystery. He was a man of great parts, of outstanding talents, born in a time of change and meanness, and without the nobility of soul necessary to save him from the traffic of the age. There is no possible reason to doubt the reality of his later religion, but he left Rome to save himself from unpleasant consequences, and he took Holy Orders in order to earn a competence.

There is a considerable amount of indirect evidence that, despite his gifts, Donne was not held in any great esteem by the ecclesiastics of his time. The splendid outstanding figure of the Church of England at the beginning of the seventeenth century was Lancelot Andrewes, a saint with the humour that saints have often possessed, a great preacher, a man of conspicuous judgment and discretion of whom Wakeman has said: 'The shaft of envy and the tongue of malice were paralysed in the presence of that serene and transparent life and the angry waves of passion were stilled in turbulent England until the gracious servant of God and the Church had passed to his rest.' To Andrewes, as to his contemporary Laud, the Church of England was, as it was to the Tractarians and is to their successors, the Catholic Church in England, and he was eager to preserve Catholic teaching and

Catholic practice. He himself said Mass in his private chapel with lights and incense, with mixed chalice and wafer bread. But he had the typical Church of England toleration for comprehensiveness and exacted nothing more than decent reverence in the churches of the three dioceses which he ruled in succession. Andrewes was lecturing at Oxford at the time when Donne was an undergraduate, and in 1608 the two men were on terms of some intimacy. Donne refers to the Bishop as his 'very learned friend,' who on one occasion lent him a book which the rabble of children at Mitcham tore to pieces. But there is no evidence that the intimacy continued. Andrewes was one of the judges who tried the nullity suit brought by the Countess of Essex as an incident of her intrigue with Rochester. Being a good and a just man he was naturally opposed to the application, though he remained silent and did not actually vote against the decision. Sir Edmund Gosse suggests that he was probably moved to admiration by Donne's clever pleading, but it is far more likely that such a man would have been horrified, and it certainly seems a fair suggestion that it was at this time that the friendship came to an end.

Abbott, the Archbishop of Canterbury, was equally horrified by the Rochester scandal and unquestionably regarded Donne's conversion with suspicion. He did what he could to hinder his preferment in the Church, and was not present at his installation as Dean of St. Paul's. Abbott was the antithesis of Lancelot Andrewes and of his predecessor, Richard Bancroft, of whom Clarendon said that he 'had almost rescued the Church out of the hands of the Calvinist party.' Abbott was a

Calvinist, stern, narrow-minded, dull and genuinely pious. On occasion he was not above truckling for the royal favour, and he played an ugly part, at King James's order, in the burning of Legget and Wightman, two Arian heretics. But the nullity suit was too much for him. The King might order, but he would have no hand in the dirty business. 'I could not force my conscience,' he said, 'which had cried upon me that it was an odious thing before God and man to give the sentence the King desired without better warrant.' Abbott is not an attractive character, but he was consistent within his own narrow lines, and his obvious antipathy to Donne was both characteristic and creditable.

William Laud was promoted from the deanery of Gloucester to the Bishopric of St. David's in the year that Donne was appointed to St. Paul's and five years later he was Bishop of Bath and Wells, Dean of the Chapel Royal, the dominant ecclesiastical figure of the royal Court. No personality in English history has been more persistently maligned than William Laud. He is the bogy man of religious Puritans and political Radicals, and everything is remembered of him except that the poor wept when he was taken from Lambeth to the Tower. Sir Edmund Gosse admits that Laud disliked Donne and suggests that the dislike was founded on jealousy of his popularity, since his orthodoxy could not be doubted. Of this, indeed, I am by no means certain, and if the orthodoxy were established, the worldliness was still further established. Laud judged quickly and surely from a very definite point of view. He had no taste for flattery. Clarendon says that 'he did court persons too little nor cared to make his designs appear as candid as they were.' He must have been perfectly familiar with the incidents of Donne's life, of the abandonment of Roman Catholicism for which Laud had far greater respect than for the Calvinism which it was his life's work to fight. He must have known about the long years in ante-rooms, seeking some secular job or the other – perhaps an embassy, or perhaps a secretaryship. He must have known of the late ordination when every other means of employment was unavailable, and of the black incident of the Essex trial. Such a Churchman must naturally have been antipathetic to a man with Laud's exalted view of the Church and the priesthood, and it is surely foolish to attribute a natural and proper dislike to jealousy. It seems clear that Charles I who, unlike his father, was a man of decent living with a rooted objection to indecent persons, shared Laud's dislike.

The point of real interest in the life of John Donne, apart altogether from his distinction as a man of letters, is that it proved that so far as the English Church was concerned the Reformation had entirely failed. It was the charge against the pre-Reformation Church that its bishops were worldlings and that its priests were too often indifferent and immoral. The justice of the charge was sadly admitted by Colet and Erasmus, and it is not to be denied that the paganism of Renaissance Rome, with its repercussions all through Europe, created the atmosphere which made the success of the Reformation possible. But while allegiance to the Pope had been repudiated in England and an intimate and essentially evil connection had been established between the Church and the head of the State, and while a comprehensiveness had been established which permitted men who held

Catholic doctrines and men who repudiated them to belong to the same body, the grievous evils of the fifteenth century were still flourishing in the seventeenth. The worldling could still find in the Church pleasant and profitable employment; pluralism and absenteeism still flourished, and John Donne collected livings with the enthusiasm and success of an earlier age. Moreover, the prelates of the reformed Church were eager in their subservience to a foolish and vicious king to an extent which would have outraged the great mediæval ecclesiastics.

It is possible to recognize the reality of Donne's religion at the end of his life without attempting the claims of his eulogists, by whom he is counted among the ornaments of the English Church, and to whom he is admirable 'as a poet, as a divine, as a metaphysician, as a humanist, and not less as a fragile and exquisite human being.' Fragile morally, he certainly was; but it is difficult to discover the exquisiteness of his character either in the gentle pages of Izaak Walton or the elaborate biography of Sir Edmund Gosse. Humanist he certainly was not, at least in the sense that Colet was a humanist, and the least said about him as a divine, the better. He went into the Church to gain a livelihood, and the Church saved him from the penury that had been the curse of his life.

Donne was a brilliant man of letters and his sermons were naturally far above the average, but their tone is suggested by contemporary criticisms. Thus of the sermon that he preached at the accession of Charles I it was said: 'Dr. Donne made them a dainty sermon upon Proverbs xxii. 11; and was exceedingly liked generally, the rather that he did Queen Elizabeth right and held himself close to the text without flattering the time too much.' Colet, it will be remembered, was generally concerned to preach sermons that could be understood by the multitude. Donne's sermons may have been all that Sir Edmund Gosse claims for them in his hyperbolical sentence, 'His hearers borne along upon the flow of his sinuous melody, now soft and winning, now vehement in storm, now piercing like a clarion, now rolling in the meditative music of an organ, felt themselves lifted up to Heaven itself.' But he had no comfort 'to speak to clouted shoon.'

Donne, indeed, was the artist in the pulpit, something of an actor, for he could weep when necessary, not insincere, properly castigating vice and extolling virtue, dominating his audience by his personality and artistry, but, as it seems to me, never a messenger of the Most High. It is indeed as an artist, and as an artist alone, that Donne is worthy of remembrance.

It is remarkable that in the years immediately preceding the Puritan revolution English literature should have been mainly distinguished by the writing of religious poetry of a high order of beauty by men entirely opposed to the doctrines and practice of the Puritans. The miscalled metaphysical poets — Vaughan, Herbert, Crawshaw, Donne — were all Catholic in their religious bias and Cavalier in their politics. Herbert was among Donne's friends, but there was little in common between the Dean of St. Paul's and his younger literary contemporaries.

Practically none of Donne's poems were printed until after his death, and it is not unreasonable to suppose that in his later years he was considerably ashamed of the eroticism of his earlier writings. Though the poems were not printed, they were obviously well-known to his contemporaries. It requires some small courage to write of Donne's poetry with critical restraint. 'Every reader of Donne,' says Professor Saintsbury, 'is either an adept or an outsider born,' and one must perforce confess oneself an outsider in agreeing with Andrew Lang that Donne is 'a poet by flashes which are very brilliant with strange coloured fires.'

THE Church of England flourished exceedingly during the reign of James II. The King's character, and the obstinate stupidity of his policy, were not good advertisements for his religion, and although conversions to Rome might properly have been expected to be a means to court favour, they were comparatively rare, and the quality of the few converts was not high. On the other hand, the reaction from Puritan restriction and Restoration excesses, combined with the high qualities of the clergy, stimulated the vitality of the English Church. Before and after the revolution, it won numbers of adherents from the ranks of dissent, and there was a remarkable development in the religious devotion of the faithful. Communions became much more numerous and frequent. Daily Masses were said in some churches. The sacrament of Penance was commonly taught – it will be remembered that Jeremy Taylor was Evelyn's director. The zeal of the laity was the result of the learning and devotion of priests and such prelates as Cosin, Jeremy Taylor, Sancroft, Ken and Kettlewell. Piety has always culminated in service, and the piety of the later seventeenth century resulted in the founding of the Society for Promoting Christian Knowledge in 1698, and the Society for the Propagation of the Gospel three years later. The renewed life of the Church was, alas, to be of the shortest duration and was soon to be lost in the formalism and materialism of the eighteenth century, but the few bright years supply an important, if brief, chapter in the history of the English Church.

It was during these years, actually in 1695, that

Jonathan Swift was ordained priest. The greater part of his clerical life was lived after the revival had spent its force, and with that revival, so far as it was spiritual, he had no part or connection, although he was to become the most effective protagonist of the political party with which the Church was to be closely identified, to its own undoing.

In 1688 Sancroft and the seven Bishops left their Sees rather than take the Oath of Allegiance to William of Orange. With them there went four hundred of the beneficed clergy, inluding Jeremy Collier. These men had been foremost in resisting the illegal demands of King James, but they were heirs of the Stuart tradition that the King was by God appointed. They could not accept the theory of the revolution that the King reigns by the will of the people, and they were too honest, too brave, perhaps too narrow-minded — many brave and good men have been very narrow-minded — to forswear themselves or to promise allegiance to a king who to them was a usurper.

With their secession, there began the sad story of the Nonjurors, a story which is the strongest warning against schism. Men of piety and learning went out into the wilderness where, except in one or two instances, they were powerless for effective service. Had they remained in the English Church, their influence and that of their successors might perhaps have saved the Church from the degradation of the early years of the Hanoverian monarchy. It is rather pathetic to remember that the last of the Nonjuror Bishops was alive when Trafalgar was fought. Though the Nonjurors eliminated themselves and became of no practical account, they established a tradition. The Catholic Churchman who held to the theory of the Church, taught by Lancelot Andrewes and for which Laud died, was inevitably associated with the Tory party, since the Nonjurors had been the victims of Whig persecution. On the other hand, the Latitudinarians, with no evangelical fervour, men with a horror of religious enthusiasm, were Whigs and extreme Erastians, welcoming the subjection of the Church to the State and eager to destroy the power of the Convocations. In the eighteenth century their influence was sufficient to damp down enthusiasm and prevent progress.

The revival may be said to have been practically destroyed in the first ten years of the eighteenth century, despite the short High Church dominance that began with the Tory Government of 1710. And it is one of the ironies with which history is replete that the principles for which the saintly Ken suffered should, twenty years later, have found their chief clerical defender in the famous Dean of St. Patrick's.

No man of genius has ever been assailed with the bitterness with which Swift has been treated by the critics of succeeding generations. To Macaulay he was a foul-mouthed, time-serving and dishonest priest; and Thackeray has summarized his character in a passage of almost unparalleled vituperation: —

'If you had been his inferior in parts (and that, with a great respect for all persons present, I fear is only very likely), his equal in mere social station, he would have bullied, scorned, and insulted you; if, undeterred by his great reputation, you had met him like a man, he would have quailed before you, and not had the pluck to reply, and gone home, and years after written a foul epigram about you — watched for you in a sewer, and come out to assail you with a coward's blow and a dirty bludgeon. If you had been a lord with a blue riband, who flattered his vanity, or could help his ambition, he would have been the most delightful company in the world. He would have been so manly, so sarcastic, so bright, odd, and original, that you might think he had no object in view but the indulgence of his humour, and that he was the most reckless, simple creature in the world. How he would have torn your enemies to pieces for you and made fun of the Opposition! His servility was so boisterous that it looked like independence; he would have done your errands, but with the air of patronizing you, and after fighting your battles, masked in the street or the press, would have kept on his hat before your wife and daughters in the drawing-room, content to take that sort of pay for his tremendous services as a bravo.'

So sweeping an indictment must be exaggerated. No man could be as bad as all that. It is remarkable that, following a twentieth-century fashion, there has not been a reaction and a bold attempt to present Swift as a devout lover, a devoted priest and a patriotic politician. In Leslie Stephen's judicial pages he is sometimes pathetic, and more often repulsive, and Mr. Charles Whibley, whose perverse affection for swashbuckling is in curious inconsistence with a kindly heart, is certainly not convincing in his short apologia. Johnson, as good a Tory and a far better Churchman, cordially disliked Swift, and it is not possible to believe that the dislike was merely due to the fact that Swift's prose was studiedly simple, while Johnson's was over-decorated, that, to use Mr. Whibley's phrase, 'one man was all for structure and the other all for ornament.' Of the greatness of Swift's genius there can be no doubt, and there can be no doubt of the twist in his character.

Jonathan Swift was born in Dublin in 1667, seven months after the death of his father, a member of a Yorkshire family who, through the good offices of a more successful brother, had been appointed steward of the King's Inn, Dublin. Swift always bitterly resented the suggestion that he was Irish because he had been born in the Irish capital, which he always hated, though in the later years of his life he became, and not unreasonably, something of an Irish hero. Most of his babyhood was spent in Whitehaven, and when he was six he was sent to Kilkenny school, which at that time enjoyed a considerable reputation, his mother having gone back to her native Leicestershire where, somehow or the other, she contrived to exist on a pension of £20 a year. Congreve was among his schoolfellows at Kilkenny, and a school friendship began between the two boys which lasted until Congreve's death. When he was fifteen, Swift was entered at Trinity, Dublin. He had already acquired the rebellious bitterness that is often the portion of the poor relation. His well-to-do uncle had lost most of his money, but Swift resented the fact that more was not done for him and declared that his uncle had given him 'the education of a dog.' His college days were embittered by a resentment which appears to have been entirely unjustified and which found its natural consequence in rebellion, often accompanied by studied insolence, against the college authorities. His career at Trinity came to an end with official censure, but he stayed on in Dublin, existing on exiguous supplies received from one or other of his relatives and apparently bitterly hating the hands that fed him.

The revolution of 1688 with the subsequent appearance of James II in Ireland, made the position of the English colony in Dublin extremely perilous and, with a group of other refugees, Swift crossed the Channel and stayed for a while with his mother in Leicester. Swift's mother was a good-tempered, resolute woman whose rather unpleasant humour once took the shape of trying to persuade her son's housekeeper, after he had become an ordained clergyman, that he was her lover and not her son. Already Swift appears to have thought of the Church as the only career likely to offer him a livelihood, and he never thought of the Church in any other way. To him, as to Donne, the Church was an income and a refuge from penury. Before his ordination he spent some years in the household of Sir William Temple, the cultured Whig statesman, at Moor Park in Surrey. Temple had played a leading part in the politics of the revolution, but he had preferred dignified retirement to the squalor of political intrigue. He was a writer of some small merit and a man of taste and feeling. Swift came into his household in his early twenties, uncouth and enormously self-assured, to act as a sort of secretary, and in the manner of the age to be treated, though doubtless always with courtesy and consideration, as a dependent and a definite inferior. To this position Swift was compelled to submit, though he resented the inferiority and was anything but grateful for the meals, the £20 a year, and the roof over his head. After a year with Temple, he went back to Ireland on account of his health. He already suffered from the painful disease of the ear which was to torture him all through his life, and which may be reasonably regarded as some excuse for his misanthropy. That he had been a useful secretary is proved by the fact that after a very short absence he was back again at Moor Park and that in 1692, owing to Temple's influence, he received the M.A. degree at Oxford. At Moor Park he met many of the statesmen who still kept in touch with Temple, among them the Earl of Portland, the Dutchman who came to this country with William, much to the advantage of himself and his descendants, and to whom on one occasion Swift gave advice with more assurance than success.

Swift began to write verse at Moor Park, verse that is actually not ineffective rhymed prose, in which he indicated that he had already determined that it was his mission to expose the follies of the age: —

'My hate, whose lash just heaven has long decreed
Shall on a day make sin and folly bleed.'

Swift expected that Temple would secure for him a fat prebendary stall if and when he took Holy Orders. But his patron was disappointing. He would make no promises, and in 1694 Swift left his employment in a temper and went back to Dublin, where he was ordained deacon in 1694 and priest in 1695, receiving from the Lord Deputy a small living worth about a hundred a year. 'Little is known of his life as a remote country clergyman,' says Leslie Stephen, 'except that he very soon became tired of it.' In 1696 he was back for the third time at Moor Park, having written before leaving Ireland a passionate love-letter to a certain Miss Waring which contains the delicate suggestion 'By Heaven, you are more experienced and have less virgin innocence than I.' Swift stayed at Moor Park until Temple's death in 1699, reading prodigiously and everything except theology. Among the inmates of Moor Park at this time was Esther Johnson, a protégée of the Temples and the Stella of the famous Journal.

Temple left Swift a legacy of £100, and at the age of thirty-one he began to rival Donne in the sordid business of seeking clerical employment. Disappointment followed disappointment, and Swift did not make his way any easier by answering disappointment with insult. 'God confound you both for a couple of scoundrels,' he said to the Earl of Berkeley and his secretary, who had promised and had not fulfilled. But at last persistence had its reward. In 1700, he obtained the living of Laracor, near Dublin, with two other small livings and a prebendary stall in St. Patrick's Cathedral, the four appointments securing him an income of £230 a year.

During his last years with Sir William Temple, Swift wrote his great satires, *A Tale of a Tub*, and *The Battle of the Books*. *A Tale of a Tub* claims to be written 'for the universal improvement of mankind.' It was warmly praised by Voltaire, who acclaimed Swift as a saner Rabelais. But as Mr. Whibley has pointed out, the comparison is misleading: 'Rabelais lived laughing and died laughing and, when he laughed the laughter of scorn, he would still be merry.' Swift rarely laughed; he never shook in an easy chair, and never laughing himself, he did not excite laughter. He would indeed be an odd and an unpleasant individual who could laugh at *A Tale of a Tub*.

'*A Tale of a Tub*,' says Professor Saintsbury, 'is one of the very greatest books in the world, one of those in which a great drift of universal thought received consummate literary form.' Queen Anne, a woman perhaps of no too great intelligence, regarded the book as utterly irreligious, but Professor Saintsbury insists that 'irreligion is neither intended nor involved in it.'

Criticism and appreciation are affected by personal prejudice. It is doubtless true that Macaulay's bitter comments on Swift were, to a large extent, inspired by the fact that Swift was a Tory and Macaulay a Whig. On the other hand, Professor Saintsbury, a Tory and a great gentleman, forgets Swift's baseness, as it would seem, because he was a Tory and writes of his achievements with exaggerated enthusiasm. Similarly, the gentle Austin Dobson's adoration of the eighteenth century and everything that belonged to it makes him present the gloomy and the grubby Dean as something of a hero.

Irony is always antipathetic to the English temperament and perhaps the one form of literary expression that is least suited to the English language. *A Tale of a Tub* is a rare achievement, but it is difficult to agree with Professor Saintsbury's estimate, and to most readers, as to Andrew Lang, the irony is heavy-handed. The main intention of the satire is to demonstrate the vast superiority of the Church of England to the Church of Rome and to Protestant dissent. The introduction is strained and mannered. The following, for example, is so deliberately ironic that it utterly fails in its effect: —

'I am so entirely satisfied with the whole present pro-
cedure of human things, that I have been for some years
preparing materials towards 'A Panegyric upon the
World'; to which I intended to add a second part,
entitled 'A Modest Defence of the Proceedings of the
Rabble in all Ages.' Both these I had thoughts to publish
by way of appendix to the following treatise; but finding
my common-place book fill much slower than I had reason
to expect, I have chosen to defer them to another occasion.'

Such a sneer, too, as that a true critic is 'a discoverer and
collector of writers' faults,' is merely trite and tiresome,
though there is definite humour – not, of course, too good-
natured – in the remark of Dryden that 'he has often said
to me in confidence that the world would have never
suspected him to be so great a poet, if he had not assured
them so frequently in his prefaces that it was impossible
that they could either doubt or forget it.'

The three religious bodies with which the satire is
concerned are represented by three brothers – Peter who,
of course, is Rome; Martin, who is the Church of England,
and Jack, who is Nonconformity. They had not been long
in the world before they fell in love with the 'Duchesse
d'Argent, Madame de Grands Titres, and the Comtesse
d'Orgeuil.' Of the Roman Church and the Roman
doctrine Swift writes with vulgar venom. For example,
here is his pleasant description of the Sacrament of
Penance: –

'A third invention was the erecting of a whispering
office for the public good, and ease of all such as are
hypochondriacal or troubled with the colic; as, likewise,
of all eaves-droppers, physicians, midwives, small politi-

cians, friends fallen out, repeating poets, lovers happy or
in despair, bawds, privy-councillors, pages, parasites and
buffoons; in short, of all such as are in danger of bursting
with too much wind. An Ass's head was placed so con-
veniently that the party affected might easily, with his
mouth, accost either of the animal's ears; which he was
to apply close for a certain space, and by a fugitive faculty,
peculiar to the ears of that animal, receive immediate
benefit either by eructation, or expiration, or evomition.'

There is an elaborate gibe at Papal Bulls, Swift con-
cluding in a burst of genuine music-hall patriotism that
'they grew at least so very troublesome to the neighbourhood that some gentleman of the North West got a parcel
of right English bull dogs and baited them so terribly
that they felt it ever after.' Another example of the
author's taste is to be found in a description of the ceremony of the kissing of the Pope's toe: —

'Peter, with much grace like a well-educated spaniel,
would present them with his foot, and if they refused his
civility, then he would raise it, as high as their chops,
and give them a damned kick on the mouth, which hath
ever since been called a salute.'

It does not seem to me an adequate defence of such
coarseness to say that men habitually wrote and spoke
in this manner two hundred years ago, for, as a matter of
fact, men of taste and feeling did not write or speak of other
people's religion in such a way two hundred years ago,
or at any other time. Swift wrote in this way because he
was a sceptic in a cassock, believing little himself,
resenting other people's faith and joying in the coarsest

and most violent bludgeoning. The reference in *A Tale of a Tub* to the Protestant Dissenters are only a little less offensive, though, perhaps, rather more humorous. After leaving their elder brother, Martin and Jack began to make coats for themselves. Martin was careful, but Jack, the Dissenter, was impatient: —

'Being clumsy by nature, and of temper, impatient, with all, beholding millions of stitches, that required the nicest hand and sedatest constitution to extricate; in a great rage he tore off the whole piece, cloth and all, and flung it into the kennel, and furiously thus continuing his career. "Ah! good brother Martin," said he, "do as I do, for the love of God; strip, tear, pull, rent, flay off all, that we may appear as unlike that rogue Peter as it is possible; I would not for a hundred pounds carry the least mark about me, that might give occasion to the neighbours of suspecting I was related to such a rascal." But Martin, who at this time happened to be extremely phlegmatic and sedate, begged his brother of all love, not to damage his coat by any means, for he never would get such another; desired him to consider, that it was not their business to form their actions by any reflection upon Peter, but by observing the rules prescribed in their father's will. That he should remember Peter was still their brother, whatever faults or injuries he had committed; and therefore they should by all means avoid such a thought as that of taking measures for good and evil from no other rule than of opposition to him. That it was true the testament of their good father was very exact in what related to the wearing of their coats; yet it was no less penal and strict in prescribing agreement, and friend-

ship, and affection between them; and therefore, if straining a point were at all dispensable, it would certainly be
so, rather to the advance of unity, than increase of contradiction.'

Swift may have claimed to have been a good Church of
England man, but his description of his own Church as
being 'extremely phlegmatic and sedate' is hardly compli-
mentary. The constant disgruntled pessimism rare in a
man in his early twenties is indicated in the final chapter: –

'Cant and vision are to the ear and the eye, the same
that tickling is to the touch. Those entertainments and
pleasures we most value in life, are such as dupe and play
the wag with the senses. For if we take an examination
of what is generally understood by happiness, as it has
respect either to the understanding or the senses, we
shall find all its properties and adjuncts will herd under
this short definition, that it is a perpetual possession of
being well deceived.'

The Battle of the Books concerns the controversy as to
the relative merits of the ancients and moderns which
Charles Perrault, the famous writer of fairy stories, began
in France. Swift, whose temperament always compelled
him to disparage his own times, was on the side of the
ancients. Dryden had recently completed his translation
of *Virgil*. The Latin poet, according to Swift, meets his
translator wearing a helmet 'nine times too large for the
head, which appeared situate in the hinder part, even
like the lady in the lobster, or like a mouse under a canopy
of state, or like a shrivelled beau within the pent-house
of a modern periwig, and the voice was suited to the

121

visage, sounding weak and remote.' The criticism is cruel but certainly not unfair. The average modern reader will probably derive from *The Battle of the Books* considerably more amusement than from *A Tale of a Tub*.

Although when he returned to Ireland, Swift had an income sufficient to provide for his own needs, he was too poor for marriage to be for him anything but an intolerable discomfort, and Miss Waring, to whom he had addressed his early love-letters, and who was growing persistent, was finally disposed of in an insulting letter in which he politely suggested that the lady did not wash sufficiently to satisfy his taste.

In 1701 Swift persuaded Esther Johnson, with her friend Mrs. Dingley, to settle in Ireland. The story of Swift and Stella has been persistently misrepresented. That a very beautiful and attractive girl should have loved a diseased and unamiable man, much her senior, is not remarkable, since beauty is constantly falling in love with the beast. That, in the circumstance, most of Stella's life was unhappy was inevitable, but despite Thackeray, it is quite clear that Swift behaved to her with considerable chivalry, and was always careful for her good name.

Following accepted custom, Swift was the absentee incumbent of Laracor. He apparently had some love for his garden, but he loathed the neighbourhood, and he contrived to spend most of his time either at Dublin Castle or in London, where he acted for a while as an agent for the Church of Ireland. In London, through the good graces of his old schoolfellow, Congreve, he met most of the literary celebrities of the time, and became intimate with Addison and Steele. But Swift was not a man who could ever mix. He was too scornful and too self-satisfied. He was bored by literary society, and he declared that he had heard at Wills's Coffee House 'the worst conversation I ever heard in my life.' Association with his fellows only added to Swift's rancour. He was the victim of envy, malice and all uncharitableness. Addison was his junior, but he obtained a comfortable official position. Other men of far less merit had secured positions which ensured a decent income, while for him there was 'nothing but the good words and wishes of a decayed Ministry.'

Swift's political position is peculiarly interesting. Born a Protestant in Ireland and coming under the influence, in his early years, of Sir William Temple, he was naturally a Whig. He was vehement in his anti-Jacobitism, despising the Stuarts for their futility, and not the less because they were Roman Catholics. One of the few genuine passions in Swift's life was his hatred of Rome. To him the revolution was the defence of the Church of England against Roman aggression, and in so far as the Tories had opposed the revolution and yearned for the return of the Stuarts, he was their convinced opponent. There is indeed a certain truth in the statement that he was a good Church of England man, though to say, as Leslie Stephen says, that he was 'as staunch a Churchman as Laud,' is a ridiculous libel on the martyred archbishop. Swift had no vocation and no real religion. His appreciation of the meaning of the priesthood is shown by the fact that he urged Gay, that most worldly of poets, to take Holy Orders in order to gain an income. But just as the Devil sometimes quotes Holy Scripture, so even the unbeliever and the worldling have often had a queer inverted loyalty to the Church.

Swift hated the Roman Church, and the Dissenter and the Presbyterian little less, and because they were non-episcopalians, Scotsmen and Dutchmen were his particular aversion. He could hardly mention the word Scotsman without adding to it the adjective damnable, and here may be found one of the few points of resemblance between the two great literary men of the eighteenth century — Swift and Johnson. It was his dislike of the Dutch which induced him to oppose the alliance with Holland which was part of the policy of Marlborough, designed to destroy French dominance on the Continent, and despite his early prejudice, Swift grew more and more in sympathy with the Tories, who were the peace party, and more and more opposed to the Whigs, who were the war party. In view of the later developments of political parties, it is interesting to note that at the beginning of the eighteenth century, war was supported by the commercial classes and opposed by the landowners and the Church.

At the end of the reign of King William, the Tories were dominant in the House of Commons, and the Whigs dominant in the House of Lords, and Swift began his career as a political pamphleteer with the publication of *A Discourse on the Dissensions in Athens and Rome* which was so vehement a defence of the Whig lords that it was generally attributed to Burnett. This pamphlet brought him compliments and a certain cheap patronage from the Whig leaders, but nothing more substantial, and association with them became difficult for him when the Tories in the House of Commons passed a bill against what was called 'occasional conformity,' the habit of certain ambitious Nonconformists who availed themselves of the

Church of England sacraments in order to obtain office while never really submitting to the Church. Moreover, he was irritated by the continuance of Whig promises without fulfilment.

In 1708 he intrigued for the vacant bishopric of Waterford, and failed. A few months later, he applied for the position of secretary to the Embassy in Vienna and was refused, and he grew more definitely anti-Whig when Lord Wharton, a man of evil life, and a Whig with developed anti-Church prejudice, was appointed Lord Lieutenant of Ireland. At this time Swift wrote his *Arguments against Abolishing Christianity*, and his *Sentiments of a Church of England Man*. In the first he adopts the Manichean position that men can be made moral by Act of Parliament. Religion can be made fashionable 'by the power of the administration,' and to make it fashionable is really all that is necessary. This, by the way, was very much the faith of the comfortable Churchman of the Victorian era. The ironic note of this pamphlet may be gathered from the following extracts: –

'For the rest, it may perhaps admit a controversy whether the banishing of all notions of religion whatsoever would be convenient for the vulgar. Not that I am in the least of opinion with those who hold religion to have been the invention of politicians to keep the lower part of the world in awe, by the fear of invisible powers; unless mankind were then very different to what it is now: for I look upon the mass or body of our people here in England to be as free-thinkers, that is to say, as staunch unbelievers, as any of the highest rank. But I conceive some scattered notions about a superior power to be of singular use for the common people, as furnishing excellent materials to keep children quiet when they grow peevish, and providing topics of amusement in a tedious winter-night. . . . Upon the whole, if it shall still be thought for the benefit of church and state that Christianity be abolished, I conceive, however, it may be more convenient to defer the execution to a time of peace, and not venture, in this conjuncture, to disoblige our allies, who, as it falls out, are all Christians, and many of them, by the prejudices of their education, so bigoted as to place a sort of pride in the appellation. If, upon being rejected by them, we are to trust to an alliance with the Turk, we shall find ourselves much deceived: for, as he is too remote, and generally engaged in war with the Persian Emperor, so his people would be more scandalized at our infidelity than our Christian neighbours. For the Turks are not only strict observers of religious worship, but, what is worse, believe a God; which is more than is required of us, even while we preserve the name of Christians.

'To conclude: whatever some may think of the great advantages to trade by this favourite scheme, I do very much apprehend that, in six months time after the act is passed for the extirpation of the gospel, the Bank and the East India stock may fall at least one *per cent*. And since that is fifty times more than ever the wisdom of our age thought fit to venture for the preservation of Christianity, there is no reason we should be at so great loss, merely for the sake of destroying it.'

The *Sentiments of the Church of England Man* are the sentiments of an Erastian.

Swift exasperated the Whigs by defending legislative

restrictions for the Nonconformists, and further indication that he was done with Whiggery and had become a whole-hearted Tory is to be found in another pamphlet published in 1708 in which he defends the Test Acts. This pamphlet was published anonymously in order to conceal the true identity of the writer from the Whig ministers who even at the eleventh hour might haply provide him with preferment. It is indeed suggested in the text that Dr. Swift himself was in favour of the abolition of religious tests. But Swift had a style of his own and the authorship was more than suspected. Any hope of preferment from Whiggery had come to an end, and Swift was characteristically violent in his reference to the men who had resented his attempt to stab them in the back.

In 1710 Queen Anne, herself a good Tory and High Churchwoman, plucked up sufficient courage to dismiss the Duchess of Marlborough, and after a General Election, which returned a Tory majority to the House of Commons, to appoint a Tory Administration with Harley and St. John at its head. The popular weariness of the war was the main cause of the fall of the Whigs, but the Church had been intimately concerned. The Whig ministers had officially impeached Dr. Sacheverell, whom Wakeman describes as 'a blatant and pompous High Churchman' for preaching seditious sermons. The Doctor was convicted, but received only a nominal sentence, which made him something of a popular martyr, and his subsequent triumphant progress through the country considerably helped to ensure the Tory victory at the polls.

Swift came to England from Ireland just before the General Election. The Whig leaders, anticipating defeat, and regretting the loss of Swift's trenchant pen, were eager to conciliate him. He was flattered and treated to expensive dinners, but he was not the man to ally himself with a falling dynasty. The Tory leaders were equally civil, and at this time their friendship was likely to be infinitely more profitable. Harley, who died Earl of Oxford, was one of those plotting mediocre politicians who by persistence frequently succeed in the House of Commons, and die in the House of Lords. At the beginning of his administration he owed an immense debt to an absurd Frenchman who tried to stab him with a pocket-knife, and thus made him a national hero, and Pope wrote for him a hyperbolic epitaph: —

> 'A soul supreme in each hard instance tried,
> Above all pain, all passion, and all pride,
> The rage of power, the blast of public breath,
> The lust of lucre, and the dread of the death.'

Henry St. John, soon to be Lord Bolingbroke, was a man of far more brilliant gifts. He was the friend of Pope as well as Swift, and a man of letters as well as a politician. He was good-looking, witty, eloquent, a libertine and a complete free-thinker who built a political career on a working alliance with High Churchmen. There have always been political adventurers in England. One or two of them have been canonized in popular tradition, but among them Bolingbroke is distinguished by his gallantry, his high spirits and his inability to play the hypocrite with much success or for very long. It was definitely to the advantage of Swift to cultivate Harley and St. John, and it was definitely to their advantage to cultivate him. The alliance on both sides was dictated by policy.

Swift, who never failed in self-appreciation, realized at once how valuable he was to the Ministry, and behaved to the new ministers with an arrogance that must have been exceedingly difficult to endure. None the less, political relations led to friendship, which lasted long after the few years of power and influence had come to an end. Writing of Swift in his years of eclipse, Bolingbroke said: —

'I loved you almost twenty years ago: I thought of you as well as I do now, better was beyond the power of conception, or to avoid an equivoque, beyond the extent of my ideas. . . . While my mind grows daily more independent of this world, and feels less need of leaning on external objects, the ideas of friendship return oftener, they busy me, they warm me more. Is it that we grow more tender as the moment of our great separation approaches? Or is it that they who are to live together in another state, for *vera amicitia non nisi inter bonos*, begin to feel that divine sympathy which is to be the great bond of their future society? There is no one thought which soothes my mind like this.'

Swift made few friends, but the friendship, that he refused to the many, was vastly valued by the few privileged few. It was not the smallest of the tragedies of his life that he could never warm his soul with the affection that was offered to him.

While he was still attached to the Whigs, Swift had shown his ability as a journalist by his contributions to Steele's *Tatler*, and in admitting Swift into the inner circle of the Government, Harley and St. John were, as Leslie Stephen says, 'paying homage to the rising power of the

I

pen.' From the autumn of 1710 to the summer of 1711,
Swift contributed a weekly article to the Tory *Examiner*,
which included among its other contributors the poet
Prior, and Atterbury, afterwards Bishop of Rochester.
Atterbury became one of Swift's associates. He was
frequently at his house in Chelsea, and his name often
appears in the *Journal to Stella*. Atterbury was himself
something of a swashbuckler and a good deal of an
adventurer, but he at least stood for definite ecclesiastical
principles to which he was faithful all his life, and for
which he ultimately paid with persecution and exile. He
had led the fight of the Lower House of Convocation in
1700 against the Whig bishops, and soon after the accession of Queen Anne, he was appointed Dean of Carlisle.
He wrote the speech which Sacheverell read at his trial,
and he had a good deal to do with the agitation that
brought the Whig Ministry to an end. In 1711 he was
made Dean of Christ Church, and in 1713 Bishop of
Rochester. He was an utter failure as a Dean, and it was
cynically said that this was the chief reason for his preferment. If Queen Anne had lived and the Tories had
remained in power, Atterbury might well have been
Archbishop of Canterbury. In the last year of Anne's life,
in common with most of the Tories, Atterbury coquetted
with Saint Germain, but he took the Oath to George I,
though the coldness of the new Government made him
its persistent and reckless critic in the House of Lords.
In 1715 he refused to sign with the other Bishops a declar-
ation of fealty to the Protestant succession, and in 1721
he was arrested for plotting with the Jacobites. A Bill
was passed by Parliament depriving him of his dignities,
and banishing him for life. He lived for twelve years in

exile, suffering that common series of humiliations that was the lot of all the faithful partisans of the Stuarts. Atterbury was a pugnacious prelate with a far greater concern for politics than religion, but he was a man of many friends, and between him and his only daughter there was a rare and beautiful affection.

The story of the years in which Swift was associated with Harley and St. John and with Prior and Atterbury, is related in his *Journal to Stella*. Stella, with the faithful Mrs. Dingley, remained in Ireland, and Swift wrote long, intimate and oddly fascinating accounts of his daily life in London, full of trivial detail, generally irritating the reader by ignoring the bigger issues, sometimes coarse, but always illuminative. To adapt the phrase of Leslie Stephen, it is the prattle of genius. The figure of Swift emerges from it, not without human attraction or human affection, but mean, self-seeking and, on occasion, brutal. Almost the last sentence in the 'Journal' is, 'I mightily approve Ppt's project of hanging the blind parson.' To me this finale gives the note of the 'Journal,' and of the man.

Religion is of the smallest interest to him. I find such entries as: 'This is Good Friday you must know, and I must rise and to Mr. Secretary about some business.' 'I was early with the Secretary to-day but he was gone to his devotions and to receive the Sacrament; several rakes did the same; it was not for piety but employments.' And again, 'I wish you a merry Lent. I hate Lent; I hate different diets, and furmity and butter and herb porridge; and sour devout faces of people who only put on religion for seven weeks.'

On fine Sunday mornings the future Dean went to church. When it was wet, he apparently stayed at home, anticipating a Victorian custom. When the Bishop of Bristol was made Lord Privy Seal, he expressed his view of the relations of Church and State by writing to Stella: 'The Whigs will fret to death to see civil employment given to a clergyman. It was a very handsome thing in my Lord Treasurer and will bind the Church to him for ever.' On one occasion Swift relates that he read prayers for a sick man, and it never seems to have occurred to him that the sick man needed confession, absolution or ghostly advice, or that he should take him the Blessed Sacrament.

Swift came from Ireland to London, an adventurer in search of fortune, the penniless man of letters in search of a patron. But he had resented the patronage of Sir William Temple and he still resented patronage. He wrote in the 'Journal': –

'I find all rich fellows have that humour of using all people without any consideration of their fortunes; but I will see them rot before they shall serve me so. Lord Halifax is always teazing me to go down to his country house, which will cost me a guinea to his servants, and twelve shillings coach hire; and he shall be hanged first.'

The Whigs snubbed him. 'But who the devil cares what they think? Am I under obligation in the least to any of them all? Rot 'em, for ungrateful dogs; I will make them repent their usage before I leave this place.' And when the Tories were friendly he suspected their friendship: 'I believe never any thing was compassed so soon, and purely done by my personal credit with Mr. Harley, who is so excessively obliging, that I know not what to make of it, unless to show the rascals of the other party that they used a man unworthily, who had deserved better.'

For the first few mcnths Swift appears to have regretted the old friends, despite the fact that they had entirely failed to help him, and to have wondered whether, after all, he had not backed the wrong horse. He wrote to Stella in 1711 : —

'As for my old friends, if you mean the Whigs, I never see them, as you may find by my journals, except Lord Halifax, and him very seldom; Lord Somers never since my first visit, for he has been a false deceitful rascal. My new friends are very kind, and I have promises enough, but I do not count upon them, and besides my pretences are very young to them.'

The political pamphleteer, however highly he may have been valued, was paid very badly in the reign of good Queen Anne, and in these London days Swift had to depend on the most meagre resources. Almost his first preoccupation every day was to 'pick up a dinner,' and it should be added that he was rarely disappointed. It did happen, however, once in the autumn of 1711. He wrote : —

'People have so left the town, that I am at loss for a dinner. It is a long time since I have been at London upon a Sunday; and the ministers are all at Windsor. It cost me eighteenpence in coach hire before I could find a place to dine in. I went to Frankland's and he was abroad; and the drab his wife looked out of window, and bowed to me without inviting me up; so I dined with Mr. Coote, my Lord Montrath's brother; my lord is with you in Ireland.'

All this is sufficiently sordid and undignified. Often, too, he had to pay for his dinner by being hopelessly bored. 'There did I sit,' he wrote, after dining with Lady Betty Germain, 'like a booby till eight o'clock looking over her and another lady at picquet when I had other business enough to do.' However he might be forced to toady, and however he might angle for his dinner, Swift contrived to keep his self-respect by an arrogance that was often positively insolent to those who gave him of their bounty. 'I sent Mr. Harley,' he wrote, 'into the House to let him know I would not dine with him if he dined late.' On another occasion, 'They called me nothing but Jonathan; and I said I believed they would leave me Jonathan as they found me and that I never knew a Ministry do anything for those whom they make companions of their pleasures; and I believe you will find it so, but I care not.' In April, 1711, he wrote: —

'I called at Mr. Secretary's to see what the D—— ailed him on Sunday; I made him a very proper speech, told him I observed he was much out of temper; that I did not expect he would tell me the cause, but would be glad to see he was in better; and one thing I warned him of, never to appear cold to me, for I would not be treated like a schoolboy; that I had felt too much of that in my life already, (meaning from Sir William Temple), that I expected every great minister, who honoured me with his acquaintance, if he heard or saw any thing to my disadvantage, would let me know in plain words, and not put me in pain to guess by the change or coldness of his countenance or behaviour; for it was what I would hardly bear from a crowned head, and I thought no subject's favour was worth it; and that I designed to let my Lord-Keeper and Mr. Harley know the same thing, that they might use me accordingly.'

As time went on, Swift began to fear, not unnaturally, that the Tories would prove to be as unsatisfactory pay-masters as the Whigs had been. It is said, indeed, that Harley had suggested to the Queen that he should be given a vacant Irish bishopric, but that having read *A Tale of a Tub*, she doubted Swift's orthodoxy and refused to confirm the appointment. 'I believe I shall die with ministries in my debt,' he wrote. And a year afterwards: — 'I have expected from one week to another that something would be done in my own affairs; but nothing at all is nor I don't know when anything will or whether, ever at all, so slow are people at doing favours.' He was always in bad health. He worked very hard, on one occasion writing three pamphlets in a fortnight. He hated the loitering in ante-chambers; he was infuriated when the Whig pamph-leteers hit back. As we see him in the 'Journal' he is much disgruntled, almost humourless.

There is this to be said to his credit, that although he had broken with the Whigs and quarrelled with Steele, he was eager to use his influence with Ministers for the benefit of his old friends, and particularly for Steele and Congreve. For Addison he had a genuine liking and regretted the passing of their intimacy. 'I believe,' he said, 'our friendship will go off by this damned business of party.' That was written in 1710, and in 1712 he wrote: 'I met Mr. Addison and Pastoral Philips on the Mall to-day and took a turn with them; but they looked terribly dry and cold. A curse on party!'

Swift was a skilled and detached observer of public affairs, and in the spring of 1711 he was perfectly convinced that peace was necessary for the country. 'This kingdom,' he wrote, 'is certainly ruined as much as was ever any bankrupt merchant. We must have peace, let it be a bad or a good one, though nobody dares talk of it. The nearer I look upon things, the worse I like them. I believe the confederacy will soon break to pieces; and our factions at home increase.' His change of party was indeed due to principle as well as to the idea of personal profit.

The life of the Tory Ministry was constantly threatened. Harley, who was soon to become Lord Oxford, was easy-going, and a bad party manager. The Queen's loyalty to her Ministers was always doubtful, and it was not until 1713 that the peace party triumphed and that the Treaty of Utrecht was signed. A few days afterwards Swift had his reward, a none too generous one, and was appointed Dean of St. Patrick's. The initial expenses of the Deanery were estimated at £1,000, 'so that,' Swift wrote, 'I shall not be better for the Deanery these three years.' Two months later the *Journal to Stella* was brought to an end with Swift's return to Dublin.

Incidentally the 'Journal' contains curiously childish fun and many execrable puns, and Swift only gives this correspondent rare character sketches of his many acquaintances. There is one very vivid pen portrait of Bolingbroke, of whom he writes: —

'I think Mr. St. John the greatest young man I ever knew; wit, capacity, beauty, quickness of apprehension, good learning, and an excellent taste; the best orator in the House of Commons, admirable conversation, good

nature, and good manners; generous, and a despiser of
money. His only fault is talking to his friends in way of
complaint of too great a load of business, which looks a
little like affectation; and he endeavours too much to mix
the fine gentleman, and man of pleasure, with the man
of business. What truth and sincerity he may have I
know not: he is now but thirty-two, and has been Secretary above a year.'

The final triumph of the Tory peace party was largely
brought about by Swift's *The Conduct of the Allies*, written
to prove that the war and the alliance with the Dutch and
Germans against the French were against national
interests, and that England was merely pulling the chest-
nuts out of the fire for Holland. Eleven thousand copies
of the pamphlet were sold in two months, and it vastly
affected public opinion.

In his letters to Stella, Swift had continually declared
his boredom with London and his desire to return to
Ireland, but he had not been in Dublin more than a few
weeks when he grew depressed and 'horribly melancholy,'
and this though he was now near the woman for whom he
had professed so great regard. The explanation is perhaps
to be found in the 'Journal,' where there are constant
references to dining with Mrs. Vanhomrigh, although
there is never any reference to the existence of her
daughter.

The glamour of the Peace of Utrecht too soon wore off,
and by October, 1713, the Ministry was again in trouble,
and urgent messages were sent to Swift to come back to
London. Oxford and Bolingbroke had quarrelled, the
Queen was ill, and the one subject of interest was the

succession. Each of his patrons had had secret com-
munication with the Pretender, and as is, of course, well
known, the Queen herself was eager that her brother
should succeed to the throne. Swift was never deluded by
the Jacobite dream. He never believed that there was a
considerable Jacobite party in England or that another
Roman Catholic sovereign would be accepted by the
English people. His political philosophy is set out in
a pamphlet, *Free Thoughts Upon the Present State of
Affairs*, written in 1714. He criticized the Tories for
their want of courage, and he urged that all Whigs and
Dissenters should he discharged from public office, that
the Court of Hanover should be warned not to intrigue
with the Whigs, and that the Heir Presumptive should
come to England. This pamphlet had been preceded
by others, one a fierce attack on Bishop Burnet, and
another, an even more venomous assault on Steele, of
whom Swift wrote: 'Do him a good turn and he is your
enemy for ever.'

So far as his mission to London was intended to recon-
cile Oxford and Bolingbroke, it was a complete failure,
and on the death of Queen Anne, Swift, anticipating
political complications, hurried back to Dublin. Swift
carefully kept away from the intrigues that followed the
arrival of George I in England, and escaped the fate of his
friends, Bolingbroke and Atterbury. For ten years he was
content to be just the Dean of St. Patrick's, and, Protestant
though he was, he contrived to earn the goodwill of the
people among whom he lived. He hated all Scotsmen
and perhaps the Scotsmen in the north of Ireland most of
all. He was mostly concerned for the prosperity of the
English settlers in southern Ireland. For the Irish, them-

selves, he had a half contemptuous affection. If they were
dull and ignorant, that was the inevitable result of slavery.
The ordinary English statesman had no thought for Ireland except for the money that could be got out of it, and
the result was that there was hardly an Irish farmer who
could 'afford shoes or stockings to his children or to eat
fish or drink anything better than sour milk and water
twice in the year.' The Irish, Swift declared, had been
'reduced to a worse condition than the peasant in France
or the vassals in Germany or Poland.'

In 1724, fate gave Swift another opportunity to write
an effective political pamphlet, and incidentally to startle
the English Government by proving that the great man
whom they had forgotten was still alive and vigorous.
A patent for supplying Ireland with a copper coinage had
been granted to the Duchess of Kendal, one of the German favourites whom George I had brought from Hanover. She was 'tall and lean of stature and had been at
once nicknamed "the Maypole" by the irreverent London
Mob.' The Duchess sold her patent to one Walter Wood,
for £10,000. The Irish Parliament protested that the
patent had been obtained by false representation. In his
Drapier's Letters, Swift attacked the whole transaction
with vigorous but utterly fallacious arguments, which
did not affect the main part of the indictment, which was
that Wood was making many thousands of pounds out
of the poverty of the Irish. These letters show Swift at
his best, and at his worst. The argument is childish, but
he was fighting for a righteous cause. His hitting was
clean and accurate and hard, and the letters made this
Englishman an Irish idol. He was acclaimed as he
walked through the streets of Dublin. The bells were

rung when he returned from a trip to England. He was something of a king in the place which he hated from the bottom of his heart, 'wretched Dublin in miserable Ireland.'

Swift paid two more visits to England, once in 1726, and again in 1727, staying with his friend Pope, and being presented to Walpole, from whom he tried, not unnaturally in vain, to secure English preferment. Returning in 1727, he never left Ireland again. He was realist enough to know that he could hope for nothing more. He was sixty and definitely on the shelf. He was in constant pain and grew ever more embittered. In 1725 he printed what is perhaps the most effective of all his pamphlets, *A Modest Proposal for Preventing the Children of Poor People in Ireland From Being a Burden to Their Parents or Country*. This is one of the most ferocious examples of irony in any language. There are too many children in Ireland. The Irish people are hungry, therefore common sense dictates that they should eat their children.

When Swift came to England in 1726, he brought the manuscript of *Gulliver's Travels* with him, and the greatest and most famous of his books was published anonymously in 1727. 'I believe,' said Arbuthnot, 'it will have as great a run as John Bunyan,' and the prophecy has not proved false. It is its author's masterpiece and, as one of the standing best sellers of the nursery library, it has become Mr. Bowdler's greatest achievement.

It is one of the most ironic circumstances in literary history that *Gulliver's Travels*, in its latter part at least, the most brutal disgusting satire ever written, should have become a nursery classic. Its author may have intended to excite shame and anger. He has, during two centuries, earned the guerdon of children's laughter. *Gulliver's Travels*, as Leslie Stephen says, is one of the few books that every one who reads at all may be assumed to have read. I am not quite sure that this is as true as it was twenty-five years ago. A generation that does not read the Bible and is unfamiliar with the story of Moses and the Bulrushes, probably knows little of Gulliver's adventures among the Lilliputians. It is to be noted of *Gulliver's Travels*, that while the first half is light-handed and witty in its irony, the later portions are repulsive, and it is suggested by his biographers that this is due to the fact that before the book was completed, sorrow and gloom had gathered round Swift and had added to his bitterness and to his misanthropic attitude to life. This may be so, but the gloating over disgusting incidents which abounds in the account of the Yahoos, is not to be accounted for by sorrow and disappointment, nor is it fair to say that in this Swift was merely the child of his age. Indeed, he disgusted his contemporaries as he has disgusted posterity. Foul is the only adjective to be applied to part four of *Gulliver's Travels*.

Swift was a good hater and he generally hated things that are hateful. He hated the shams of politics and the shams of religion; he hated war and pretence and oppression. He hated, that is, all the things that Dickens and every other good humanist have hated. But while Dickens laughed at an evil world and laughed it cleaner, Swift stormed and denounced and jeered; and while Dickens saw that good existed with evil and that mankind was intrinsically splendid and savable, Swift saw nothing but the evil and was at last convinced that his fellow-man was just a Yahoo. 'Expect no more from man,' he says, 'than such an animal is capable of.'

Swift, a Dean of the English Church, arrived at the end of his life at a point of view that is the antithesis of the Christian religion. He denounced everything that Christianity affirms, and to submit that his view of life is supported by human experience is merely puerile. Fools there have always been in the world, and self-seekers, and now and again perhaps an odd unconscionable villain. But in every generation kind hearts have contrived to exist with coroneted heads, while in every generation the lives of simple people, sometimes spent in mean streets, are so consistently instinct with unselfish sweetness and attractive devotion as to establish man's right to be numbered with the children of God, and to make it quite certain that after much travail he will be worthy to stand within the Beatific Vision. The pessimism of Swift, shared as it often is by far lesser men, is sheer stupidity, the result of conceit, hardened by disappointment and sometimes, as was at least partly true in Swift's case, of continuous physical disease. No man can possibly believe that his fellows are Yahoos unless his brain is addled or his heart a stone. Optimism or, as a philosophic Tory would call it, sentimentalism, was not the characteristic of the eighteenth century, but Swift went farther than his contemporaries in his contempt for his kind. And the intellectual contempt of the age of Swift and Voltaire had its proper and necessary consequence, the guillotine on the Place de la Revolution.

It is possible that Swift had in mind More's *Utopia* and Bunyan's *Pilgrim's Progress* when he sat down to write *Gulliver's Travels*. Hazlitt has said: —

'He endeavoured to escape from the persecution of realities into the regions of fancy, and invented his Lilliputians and Brobdingnagians, Yahoos, and Houynhyms, as a diversion to the more painful knowledge of the world around him: *they* only made him laugh, while men and women made him angry. His feverish impatience made him view the infirmities of that great baby the world, with the same scrutinizing glance and jealous irritability that a parent regards the failings of its offspring.'

Hazlitt is here too kind. There was nothing of the attitude of a parent in Swift. His was rather the scorn of the one wise man for the generation of fools with whom he was concerned. Leslie Stephen says: —

'Swift's satire is congenial to the mental attitude of all who have persuaded themselves that men are, in fact, a set of contemptible fools and knaves, in whose quarrels and mutual slaughterings the wise and good could not persuade themselves to take a serious interest. He "proves" nothing, mathematically or otherwise. If you do not share his sentiments, there is nothing in the mere alteration of the scale to convince you that they are right; you may say, with Hazlitt, that heroism is as admirable in a Lilliputian as in a Brobdingnagian, and believe that war calls forth patriotism, and often advances civilization. What Swift has really done is to provide for the man who despises his species a number of exceedingly effective symbols for the utterance of his contempt.'

This seems to me quite admirable, and it also seems a terrible misuse of genius to supply effective symbols to the pompous asses who despise their species. Magnitude

of achievement cannot reasonably be counted as the justification for evil conduct or outrageous philosophy. It is
not improbable that the splendid sinner admired for his
audacity even by the virtuous on earth, may cut a pitiful
figure on the Judgment Day.

Gulliver's Travels is a unique work of genius. We all
owe Swift a debt for at least half of it, for the lashing of
folly and the protest against oppression, for the wit and
for the delightful smooth narrative. But it is not true that
the repulsion for Swift, expressed perhaps with an unnecessary wealth of adjectives by Thackeray, is due to the
resentment of the ordinary individual against the person
who tells unpleasant truths. Swift's offence is that he tells
unpleasant lies, and the repulsion that he excites is due to
the fact that the normal man properly regards contempt as
the most horrible of all sins. It is good to love, and it may
be good to hate; it is good to pity, it is good to laugh, but
to despise is the utmost damnation. And Swift, disgruntled genius as he was, by his sheer eminence compels
recognition of the fate that awaits him who despises his
fellows. It is an evil thing to take a hammer and shiver to
pieces a fine marble statue; it is a much worse thing to
fill a bucket from the kennels and plaster over the beautiful statue with unspeakable filth. And that is exactly what
Swift did. 'We should,' says Leslie Stephen, 'be rather
awed and repelled by this spectacle of a nature of magnificent power struck down, bruised and crushed under fortune and yet fronting all antagonists with increasing pride
and comforting itself with scorn even when it can no
longer injure its adversaries.' But the picture is over-
drawn. Swift was a disappointed man, but he had
received considerable preferment in the only Christian

Church in the world that would have tolerated him.
Certainly his courage was unbreakable, but can it be
suggested that we should be 'awed' by the repayment
of the world's ingratitude by flinging the Yahoo in its
face.

Gulliver's Travels was the last, as it was the greatest, of
Swift's writing. During the remainder of his life, he
continued in Dublin, caring for the poor in a particularly
practical manner, quarrelling with the bishops, writing
letters characterized by a singularly doleful form of
humour. One of his last was the poem on the death of
Dr. Swift, in which he prophesied: —

> 'Poor Pope will grieve a month, and Gay
> A week, and Arbuthnot a day,
> St. John himself will scarce forbear
> To bite his pen and drop a tear,
> The rest will give a shrug and cry,
> "'Tis pity, but we all must die!"'

Like many another writer of genius Swift lost his
intellect some years before he died. He lived on in almost
a state of torpor until October 19, 1745.

There remains to be considered Swift's relations with
the two women who played any considerable part in his
life, Stella and Vanessa. A man's relations with women,
and particularly with the women that he chooses for his
intimates, must obviously be illuminative of his character,
and therefore not to be disregarded, despite Mr. Whibley's
reference to those critics of Swift 'who with something of
the eavesdropper's impertinence would pierce the mystery
of his loves.'

It is a truism of experience that the passionless woman

is often the most persistent of philanderers. Men are probably less frequently passionless than women, but when they are so limited — or may be blest — they will commonly be found to have the same desire to linger and to lean over the gate which they have no intention of opening. The explanation of the relations between Swift and Stella and Vanessa, and of the earlier incident with Varina, is to be found in his temperament. He liked gossiping to women; he liked writing to women; he liked being admired by women; above all, he liked domineering over women. It was always necessary for him to have some obedient slave who hung on his words and eagerly responded to his every mood, but there is absolutely no indication in the 'Journal' or in his letters that he was ever in love in any sense of the phrase. The endearing messages in the 'Journal' are as often sent to Mrs. Dingley as to Stella herself, and Vanessa's outspoken passion perplexed and irritated him. Perhaps because Swift was himself great in his achievement, great in his twisted character, everything concerned with him has been grotesquely exaggerated. His political services were rewarded with a comparatively fat Deanery, but admiring biographers refer to the hardness of his lot, while his detractors suggest that a young woman who was apparently herself quite content with the circumstances of her life, was an outraged and ill-used heroine. Could anything be more absurd than Thackeray's rhapsody over Stella:—

'Gentle lady! — so lovely, so loving, so unhappy. You have had countless champions, millions of manly hearts mourning for you. From generation to generation we take

up the fond tradition of your beauty; we watch and follow
your tragedy, your bright morning love and purity, your
constancy, your grief, your sweet martyrdom. We know
your legend by heart. You are one of the saints of English
story.'

'Sweet martyrdom,' and 'saint,' used in this connection,
are nothing but the grotesqueries of rhetoric. What are
the facts? As has been said, Swift first met Stella when
she was a child of eight, living in Sir William Temple's
household, and she became his pupil. When Temple
died, he very reasonably suggested that she would live
more comfortably on her small income if she left England
and settled in Ireland, where she possessed a small pro-
perty, and there she lived for the rest of her days. After
her death in 1728, Swift wrote of her as 'one of the most
beautiful and graceful and agreeable' of young women,
though he adds, with his usual candour, that she was a little
too fat. Her hair, he tells us, was 'blacker than a raven
and every feature of her face is perfection.' He had great
respect for her judgment and the deepest admiration for
her character. She was 'the truest, most virtuous and
valuable friend,' and 'never was so happy a conjunction of
civility, freedom, easiness and sincerity.' The description
is attractive. For all his deep growling at the world, for
all his outspoken hatred of humanity, Swift was hungry for
friends though he often repelled friendship and Stella was
the greatest of his friends, meaning more to him than
Bolingbroke or Arbuthnot. And that was all.

It is doubtful whether Swift ever married Stella. It is
quite certain that he had no desire for marriage. If the
wedding actually took place, he was forced into it by

circumstances. Before he was appointed to the Deanery of St. Patrick's he confessed that both his humour and his lack of means made him adverse to the idea of marriage, and although the Deanery made him far better off than most of his clerical brethren, his appointment left him disinclined to the acceptance of financial responsibility. Swift was no vulgar hoarder of money. He was, indeed, both thrifty and generous, but his early experiences and his temperament caused him to loathe the idea of dependence and to cherish personal freedom above all other things. Such freedom depended on the possession of an adequate income. As a bachelor and Dean of St. Patrick's, he need ask no man for favours, but with a wife and, maybe, a family, he might be compelled once more to the suppliance against which his rugged independence rebelled. Moreover, from his youth, Swift was a sick man. The 'Journal' is full of references to pills and pain. The disease of the ear from which he suffered must have caused him persistent agony and was no doubt the beginning of the mental trouble which darkened his last years. He was physically unfit for marriage. He probably realized that constant and intimate association with any one person, however much she were esteemed, would become intolerable to him. His position, as it seems to me, is perfectly easy to understand. It was perhaps a little pitiful, but certainly by no means unique.

Swift preferred women friends to men friends because they were more easily bullied. The brutality with which he habitually treated women – 'Pray, Madam, are you as proud and ill-natured as when I saw you last?' he once asked Lady Burlington – was perhaps, as Leslie Stephen suggests, mere affectation, but it must have been very offensive, and is, indeed, paralleled by the humiliation that Swift loved to inflict on his inferiors as when he compelled an unfortunate curate to drink sour wine. Given docility and complete subjection, Swift would, at times, respond with candid affection. Leslie Stephen finds delight in the 'playful prattle' and 'fond triflings' of the 'Journal,' but I confess that I find the 'baby talk' silly and irritating. On the other hand, the expressions of an affection that is paternal or brotherly are frequent and often sincere. 'And can Stella read this writing without hurting her dear eyes? O faith, I'm afraid not. Have a care of those eyes pray pray pretty Stella.' 'I wish my dearest pretty Dingley and Stella a happy new-year, and health, and mirth, and good stomachs, and Fr's company.' 'It will be just three weeks when I have the next letter, that's to-morrow. Farewell, dearest beloved MD, and love poor, poor Presto, who has not had one happy day since he left you, as hope saved.' And so on.

The frequent droppings into poetry, too, show a dour man at his brightest and emphasize the reality of his friendship:—

> 'Stay till night,
> And then I'll write
> In black and white,
> By candlelight
> Of wax so bright,
> It helps the sight,
> A bite a bite!
> Marry come up, Mrs. Boldface.'

And again:—

'Mr. White and Mr. Red
Write to MD when abed;
Mr. Black and Mr. Brown,
Write to MD when you are down;
Mr. Oak and Mr. Willow,
Write to MD on your pillow.'

Stella was apparently content with the friendship of the man whose greatness she had intelligence enough to realize and demanded nothing more than he was ready to give. But Vanessa was an entirely different sort of woman. Hester Vanhomrigh was seventeen when Swift began his frequent visits to her mother's house. She was something of a bluestocking and she fell head over ears in love with Swift, as Heloise had fallen in love with Abelard. Indeed, there is a suggestion of that greatest of all romances in Swift's poem *Cademus and Vanessa*. 'Vanessa loved Swift,' says Leslie Stephen, 'and Swift it seems allowed himself to be loved.' But how on earth he could have prevented her is not explained. He was doubtless flattered. He probably had little fear of possible consequences. He had merely acquired one more willing slave. Her mother died soon after Swift had settled in Dublin, and Vanessa was also persuaded to settle in Ireland in a village a few miles away from Stella, and then, of course, the trouble began. Swift was fearful that Stella, whom he obviously valued the more, would grow jealous if she discovered the relations between him and Vanessa, on whom he urged a discretion which she found intolerable. Vanessa grew more vehement in her passion and more and more resentful of what she called his 'prodigious neglect.' Her life was a 'languishing death.' Her letters are full of the hyperbole of the lovesick. She refers to Swift's 'radiant form,' and she says: 'Nor is the love I bear you only seated in my soul for there is not a single atom of my frame that is not blended with it.' And all the comfort that Swift can offer is to advise her to read 'diverting books.' He bitterly regretted that he had brought her to Ireland and urged her 'to quit this scoundrel island,' but the unhappy woman, alone and in straitened circumstances, persisted in staying on. In 1725 she wrote to Stella, bluntly asking if she was married to Swift, and Stella, possibly out of sheer feminine maliciousness, answered that she was. The marriage, by the way, is said to have taken place in 1716. Stella sent Vanessa's letter to Swift, and he was furious. He rode over to Vanessa's cottage, went into her room with glowering face, threw the letter on the table, and went out without speaking a word. And that was the last time she saw him. She died a few months afterwards, perhaps of a broken heart, but far more likely from the same disease that had killed her brothers and sister at a very early age. Swift was conscience-stricken and humiliated by the whole business, but there is no suggestion that Vanessa's death affected him in anything like the same way as Stella's death, which took place in January, 1728, and which really brought his own life to an end. Stella might have married a very ordinary clergyman and lived the harassed life of a clergyman's wife. From her own point of view she probably chose well in preferring to be the confidante of an erratic and gloomy genius.

Swift was unlucky in his relations with women, but his was the common fate of the passionless philanderer who demands a great deal and is able to give very little. It is not in the least true, as Thackeray said, that 'he shrank away from all affection.' On the contrary, his need of affection and sympathy is shown in the fact that he persuaded both the women with whom he was most intimately connected to leave England and settle near him. The trouble arose from a jealousy that he was unable to understand and which he most certainly resented, and in the one case from a demand which he was equally unable to understand and which his own limitations had prevented him from anticipating.

While he regarded the bulk of men as unworthy of anything but contempt, he had for the few whom he regarded as his equals almost exaggerated admiration. 'If the world had but a dozen Arbuthnots in it,' he wrote to Pope, 'I would burn my "Travels." ' And it was by comparison with his friends that the Yahoos appeared so entirely hateful. It is true that in his last years he shrank away from his friends, but that is to be attributed to the deep and perfectly natural melancholy that fell on a man of genius when he realized that his intellect was failing him. But in the short years of intimacy his friendship was generous and always understanding. It might have appeared that there was little in common between Swift and the light-hearted irresponsible Gay; but for Gay he had the affection of an elder brother, advising him wisely and properly appreciating his talent. For Pope he had always a generous admiration, and of all his friends Arbuthnot, as Mr. Whibley says, 'was obviously nearest his heart.'

I have already noted how eager he was to be of service to his intimates, and his kindness to struggling and talented youth is consistent with his care for the Irish poor when he had settled among them, and his fierce resentment against the injustice of which they were the victims. 'There was scarcely,' says Lecky, 'a man of genius of the age who was not indebted to him.'

Swift is of the type that the sentimentalist naturally finds intolerable. His manners were of the worst, his satire is difficult to understand, his coarseness is often disgusting. But the sentimentalist is a poor judge. Fundamentally Swift was hampered and finally damned by the contempt in which he held his fellows, but the contempt is partially explained, if it could never be justified, by a splendid hatred of injustice and meanness and folly, and was at least mitigated by a readiness to help the lame dog over the stile however deeply the dog might be despised for his lameness. Jonathan Swift was a mass of contradictions, and the contradictions were so mingled that life for him was a heartbreaking adventure. If he hated much, he suffered much. And what worse thing could happen to any man than to hate his brothers and to be a priest of the Christian Church.

ARTHUR PENRHYN STANLEY, Dean of Westminster from 1864 to 1881, may be regarded as the first and perhaps the most distinguished exponent of the doctrine that the Church of England should be comprehensive as well as established. To Stanley and to his disciples, among whom are to be reckoned a considerable portion of the present episcopate, the words 'comprehensive' and 'established' have a far greater significance and importance than the words 'Catholic' and 'Apostolic.'

Stanley was born in 1815 into the circle of the privileged elect. He was a son of the very comfortable Manse. His father, the rector of Alderley, was the brother of a peer and was himself to die a bishop, and the house in which Stanley was born was one of those old-fashioned rectories in which old-fashioned rectors with considerable private means contrived to live a pleasant and a godly life. Stanley was brought up in an atmosphere of prosperous piety, a delicate, sensitive boy who in his early childhood acquired the passion for writing letters which he retained to the end of his life. He was shy and reserved, and when he was ten, Southey was his favourite writer!

In 1829 Stanley was sent to Rugby, where Dr. Arnold had been installed as Head Master for something over a year. Stanley was considerably senior at Rugby to Tom Hughes, and his school-days began before Arnold's reforms had had much effect on school life. He appears to have succeeded in living a life apart from the rough and tumble, and he was amazed when *Tom Brown's School Days* was published. 'It is an absolute revelation to me,' he said. He never played games and he apparently was never bullied, a fact which appears to suggest that Rugby can hardly have been as black as it was painted by Tom Hughes. His school-days were indeed a triumph. He won every prize that he could win, and he gained from Arnold the commendation that prize-winning always elicits from head masters.

Stanley was certainly an amazing youth. He read prodigiously, but with a curious priggish purpose. For example, in one of his letters he says that he is reading Milton all through 'partly because it is useful for school work for the references to history, etc., in the similes and for the comparison of it with the old writers.' He read Gibbon, he read Walton, he read Byron, although he thought the poetry 'over-ripe fruit.' He read the recently published *Christian Year* which he rather quaintly described as 'midway between sacred poetry and secular poesie.' He was already something of a politician, and, according to his family tradition, favoured Whig reform, and, while he was still a schoolboy, he had read the first of those Oxford tracts which were to transform the Church of England.

From his boyhood it had been assumed that he would follow his father into the Church; but when he left Rugby he was troubled by doubts about the Articles. He decided that he did not entirely believe them and he wisely determined 'to read one of those books which I suppose exist to explain better than I can how far they can be conscientiously subscribed.' More material considerations added to his hesitation. He realized that the satisfaction of the clerical life largely depended on its circumstances, though in the nineteenth century a priest who was the nephew of a baron and the son of a bishop need have had little fear on this score.

But his greatest trouble was the Athanasian Creed, which he had learned from Arnold to detest, and both master and pupil would have shouted with decorous glee had they lived in these days when the bench of Bishops has practically thrown the Creed into the waste-paper basket. Arnold objected to it because it prevented Unitarians from joining the Church of England and thus made impossible that complete comprehensiveness which Stanley afterwards so earnestly desired. Stanley was so disturbed by the damnatory clauses that at the last moment he hesitated at offering himself for ordination. His biographer, Mr. Rowland Prothero, says that St. Athanasius, that determined 'little red-headed man,' 'darkened with a shadow of exceeding gloom the most momentous period of his life. Its effect was never obliterated by time or by experience. It exercised a marked influence on his views and actions from the days of his ordination down to the last hour of conscious life.'

Stanley acquired from Arnold much more than his horror of St. Athanasius. All through his life he adhered to the Liberal Protestantism that he was taught at Rugby, and so great was his devotion to Arnold, that he had some fear of going to Oxford lest at the University, where Arnold's pamphlet on Church reform had produced a considerable sensation, he should find himself among men who misunderstood and failed to appreciate his old Head Master. In one of his early Oxford letters he says: 'What a wonderful influence that man has had on my mind. I certainly feel that I have hardly a free will of my own on any subject about which he has written or spoken.'

Arnold is one of the pathetic figures of the early years of the Victorian era – a powerful, talented, narrow, self-satisfied man, ever impressed with the belief that an English Christian gentleman is the greatest of all God's creations – provided, that is, that he is not a Catholic and does not dislike Dissenters – almost without imagination, the creator, as Mr. Lytton Strachey has pointed out, of a school system which he himself did not desire and would hardly have understood. 'The earnest enthusiast who strove to make his pupils Christian gentlemen, and who governed his school according to the principles of the Old Testament, has been largely responsible for the worship of athletics and the worship of good form.' However, Stanley, one of the most distinguished of his pupils, certainly did not worship athletics, although he never lacked respect for good form.

In 1834 Stanley went up to Balliol. He arrived on a Saturday and on the Sunday he heard Pusey preach the University sermon on the Song of Solomon. It was only a few months before that Pusey had first associated himself with the Tractarians and had become with Keble and Newman one of the dominating figures of that most interesting of all English religious revivals, which, after nearly a hundred years, has by no means spent its force, which has had the most enormous effect on the practice and teaching of religion both in the Church of England and outside its borders, and which may yet succeed in making the Church everything which Arnold and Stanley most earnestly desired that it should not be. When Keble preached the famous Assize sermon, with which the history of the Oxford Movement began, the Church was certainly in sad need of revival and reform. The Evangelical movement of the end of the eighteenth century had run its course and had indeed had little apparent effect on the general life of the Church. The bishops were, at the best, amiable pedants, and at the worst, political world-lings. 'Of spiritual leadership,' says Wakeman, 'they had little idea.' Absenteeism and pluralities were as common as they were in the days of Donne, and far more common than they were in the days of Colet. Neither provincial nor diocesan synods ever met. The cathedrals were bare and neglected. Mass was said rarely and with little reverence; Communions were few and the churches had become almost as completely 'preaching shops' as the Nonconformist Conventicles. There was no clerical discipline, no clerical enthusiasm, and a considerable amount of clerical laxity.

Candidates for Holy Orders were casually examined in the tent of a cricket field between the innings or while the examining chaplain was shaving, and well-born candidates for the priesthood were exempt from examination altogether. The parson was often in the hunting field, rarely in the sanctuary, and never in the confessional. Again to quote Wakeman, 'They (the clergy) had no higher idea of the Church than of a human institution bound up in this country with the greatness of the nation and necessary for the preservation of that happy constitu-tion in Church and State which was believed to be the special gift of God to England. Generally the clergy taught "a negative and cold Protestantism deadening to the imagination, studiously repressive to the emotions and based on principles which found little sanction either in reason or in history." '

Both the Erastianism of Arnold and the Tractarianism of Newman were a revolt against this prevailing caricature of religion. Arnold dreamed of a Church which should include all Protestant Christians joined together by a common hatred of Eucharistic doctrine and other Popish superstitions. His position, which Stanley shared with some modifications, was very much that which is held to-day by the Dean of St. Paul's and the Bishop of Birmingham. The Tractarian movement, on the other side, was based on the conviction that the Church of England was the Catholic Church in England. It aimed at the restoration of Catholic practice, and it declared with an insistence that might well have been inherited from Becket, that the Church is by its nature independent of the State and that its laws are of far greater importance and significance than secular laws. It was this anti-Erastianism that was the subject of Keble's sermon on National Apostasy delivered in July, 1833.

Six years before, Keble had published *The Christian Year*, and in 1831 he had been elected Professor of Poetry. He was, I believe, the last of the Oxford Professors to lecture in Latin. He was a gentle, humble, retiring man, intensely religious and incidentally a first-rate scholar. Keble, like Arnold, was a Fellow of Oriel, as were Newman, Pusey and Richard Hurrell Froude. Froude had been Keble's pupil, and it was he who was responsible for the friendship between his old tutor and Newman. He was a brilliant, impulsive young man, overflowing with the zest of life, a keen reader, incapable of humbug and compromise, and a man who had adopted for himself a life of mediæval severity. Laud was his hero, and for the reformers he had nothing but loudly expressed contempt. He is reported to have said that there was nothing really good to remember of Cranmer except that he had burned well.

In 1833 Newman was thirty-two years old, nine years younger than Keble, a year younger than Pusey, two years older than Froude. He had started life as a strong Evangelical, but even before the intimacy of the Oriel common room began, he had considerably modified his opinions. He remains, perhaps, the most lovely and splendid figure of the Victorian era, a man of sorrows who triumphed through failure and gained immortality after a long journey along the road of neglect. Mr. Lytton Strachey has penned an incomparable word picture of Newman: 'He was a child of the Romantic Revival, a creature of emotion and of memory, a dreamer whose secret spirit dwelt apart in delectable mountains, an artist whose subtle senses caught like a shower in the sunshine the impalpable rainbow of the immaterial world.'

Taking Newman and Arnold as the typical representatives of the two antagonistic religious movements of the 'thirties, Newman the Romanticist, with, as Mr. Lytton Strachey has scornfully put it, 'his attachment to the writings of ancient monks,' was really the realist in his appreciation of facts, while Arnold was the sentimentalist, at least in so far as religion and the Church of England were concerned. It is an illusion, and a mischievous illusion, that incompatibles can be made compatible and that the contradictory can be made to agree. No society, secular or religious, can permanently exist if it be made up of men who differ on matters of fundamental importance. The conviction of the Tractarians was that as the Church of England is Catholic it must be Catholic in its practice with the consequence that it must be altogether Catholic. The Arnold-Stanley conviction was that the Church of England was national. Arnold would have admitted Unitarians, and if he had lived in the days of imperial expansion, he would surely have desired that the Church should extend its boundaries with the nation and that room should be found within its fold for Buddhists from India and pious Juju men from Africa. To the Catholic, the very expression National Church suggests a contradiction, and his dislike of establishment is due to some extent to the obvious fact that the comprehension is only made possible by the existence of outside secular authority. Dr. R. J. Campbell has well said of the Church of England: 'It is not one system but a congerie of mutually incompatible systems forced into an artificial conjunction by State enactment and the *vis inertiæ* of use and wont.' The Tractarians, like their successors, the Anglo-Catholics, resented State direction and resisted State aggression. The school to which Stanley belonged regarded the State connection as vital to the life of the Church and was not prepared with any very vigorous resistance to State aggression. This was shown very clearly when the Reform Government of 1832 introduced an Irish Church Bill which enacted that a number of dioceses in Ireland should be abolished and their incomes appropriated for secular purposes.

The first of the *Tracts for the Times* was published in the autumn of 1833, when Stanley was still at Rugby. The early tracts were short, were sold at a penny and were intended to teach various aspects of Catholic truth. Dr. Pusey, a well-born scholar who had been taught the doctrine of the Real Presence by his mother, signalized his adhesion to the movement by writing the tract on fasting, Number 18. He followed this with a very outspoken essay on baptismal regeneration which

L

produced almost as great a sensation as Newman's Tract No. 90. Pusey was a retiring scholar, almost as shy as Keble, and it was characteristic of him that he was never photographed in all his life. As a scholar he had an international reputation and he made something of a record by holding his chair as Regius Professor of Hebrew for fifty-four years. The character of the Oxford Movement can indeed never be understood unless it is realized that it was founded by men of outstanding distinction as scholars.

In 1828 Newman became Vicar of St. Mary's, and next to the Tracts it was his sermons in the University church that gave the movement its vitality and its influence. Dean Church says of these sermons: 'Plain, direct, unornamented, clothed in English that was only pure and lucid, free from any faults of taste, strong in their flexibility and perfect command both of language and of thought, they were the expression of a piercing and large insight into character and conscience and motives, of a sympathy at once most tender and most stern with the tempted and wavering, of an absolute and burning faith in God.

It was to this Oxford of Newman and Pusey with their teaching of 'revolutionary reaction' that Stanley went in 1834. 'A new strange notion of taking Christianity literally,' says Mr. Strachey, 'was delightful to earnest minds, but it was also alarming really to mean every word you said when you repeated the Athanasian Creed!'

'The new strange notion' must have been anything but delightful to Stanley's earnest mind, and to him it would have been alarming indeed to profess absolute belief in the Athanasian Creed. In view of the recent development of a distinctly Liberal Catholicism in the English Church, it is interesting to note that the Oxford Movement was inspired almost as much by a dread of Liberalism as of a hatred of Erastianism. The Tractarian regarded Liberalism — I quote Dean Church — as 'the tendencies of modern thought to destroy the basis of revealed religion and ultimately of all that can be called religion at all.'

Stanley was not attracted by Tractarianism and he was not particularly impressed by Pusey's sermon on the Song of Solomon. He found it 'singularly anti-rationalistic.' But he soon made acquaintances among the Tractarians. One of his early Oxford friends was Marriott, an Oriel Fellow, and one of Newman's most fervent admirers, and he became intimate with Ward and Faber, both of whom afterwards went to Rome. In his journals there are interesting descriptions of his early Oxford companions. Ward he describes as 'a huge moon-faced man,' and Keble as 'a middle-sized rather sharp-faced man with very twinkling eyes.' But never for one moment was Stanley convinced by his new friends. He was, however, the apostle of peace. He dreaded a clash between Newman and Arnold. To him they were 'of the very same essence.' Stanley never could understand why good men should not compose their differences and run in double harness. His own position was clear and unchanging. For all his friendship for Faber and Ward, and for all his admiration for the artistry of Newman's sermons, he was definitely anti-Tractarian.

The claim made by Newman and his associates that the Church of England had retained its Catholic character and privileges depended on the doctrine of the Apostolic

Succession, and it was round this doctrine that controversy
centred in Oxford in Stanley's undergraduate days.
Arnold denounced it as a mischievous superstition and
positive blasphemy, and Stanley, more politely, described
it as un-Christian and un-Anglican, a delightful combination of terms which exactly suggests his point of view and
to some extent his character.

In Stanley's second year, Oxford was disturbed by the
proposal to abolish university tests so that Nonconformists could become undergraduates without professing
loyalty to the Church of England. He, of course, was on
the side of the Nonconformists. Stanley was nothing if
not tolerant. I am not prepared to exaggerate the value
of toleration. Men who believe in nothing very much
always find it easy to be tolerant of other people's opinions
and prejudices. But it is difficult to hold to any faith with
living enthusiasm and at the same time to believe that
every other faith is of nearly equal value. The Victorian
religion of which Stanley was to become the most distinguished exponent, had no effect on the lives of average
men and women just because it lacked the quality which
makes toleration difficult. At the same time, it would be
idle to deny that the tolerant man is generally a more
charming companion than the zealot.

Stanley's sympathy with Nonconformists was as great
as that of Arnold, and unlike Arnold, he had understanding and appreciation even for Roman Catholics. After a
visit to Ireland in the long vacation of 1835, he wrote of
services that he had attended in Roman Catholic chapels:
'I can bear testimony that they kept throughout within the
limits of veneration without idolatry.' He disliked open
denunciation of the teaching of Newman, however objec-

tionable it might be to him, and he believed that Roman
Catholics and Tractarians might become fellow-workers
with good Protestants 'against our common enemy.'

The beginning of 1836 saw the intensifying of the
theological feud in Oxford. In January, 1836, Lord Melbourne appointed Dr. Hampden, Principal of St. Mary's
Hall, Regius Professor of Divinity — 'a very dry and dull
divine,' Canon Ollard calls him, not unreasonably suspected for his heretical opinions. Four years before, Dr.
Hampden had been Bampton lecturer. It is said that his
lectures were largely dictated by a Unitarian acquaintance and that the lecturer himself was so dry and dull
that he did not understand the implications of what he
had written. Stanley says that Hampden had 'the most
extraordinary faculty of writing obscurely that any man
ever had.' No one apparently knew what Dr. Hampden
meant, not even Dr. Hampden. The lectures, however,
had a definitely heretical suggestion, and the appointment
aroused a storm of protest both from the Tractarians and
from the orthodox Protestants. Newman and Pusey wrote
Tracts criticizing the theology of the Professor elect, and
even the ecclesiastical authorities were indignant and a
petition approved by the two archbishops was sent to the
king. Arnold rushed in with an article in the *Edinburgh
Review*, in which he defended Hampden and fiercely
attacked the 'Oxford malignants,' and after much storm
and stress, the University Convocation by a large majority
passed a disqualifying statute declaring that the University had no confidence in the Professor and depriving him
of his usual place on the board for the nomination of
selected preachers and on the board appointed to watch
out for heretical teaching in the University. This was a

great victory for the Tractarians, but it roused against them the bitter enmity of the Liberals and was the prelude to the attacks of the next few years. Stanley characteristically regarded the appointment of Hampden as a bad blunder and the attacks made on him as a worse. He was equally critical of Newman's and Pusey's onslaughts and of Arnold's ill-mannered defence, in which with amazing vulgarity he referred to the 'pretended holiness of the Tractarians.'

In 1837 Stanley became Ireland Scholar, won the Newdigate and took a first. His ambition was a Balliol Fellowship, but his friendship with Arnold, and the fear – this again shows the strength of the Tractarian influence – that the College might be regarded as heretical, prevented his election. This was a grievous disappointment, and although in 1838 he was elected a Fellow of University College, to him it was 'the bishopric of Man instead of the archbishopric of Canterbury.'

University reform and doubts about the Athanasian Creed were his preoccupations at this time. But at Christmas, 1839, despite St. Athanasius, Stanley was ordained Deacon.

Meanwhile the growing Liberal resentment against the Tractarian Movement had been stimulated by the publication of the diary of Hurrell Froude, who had died in 1836. It is a magnificently indiscreet and vastly entertaining autobiography, an intimate revelation of a sincere man's inner life, full of such splendid indiscretions as that 'the Reformation was a limb badly set, it must be broken down to be righted.' Canon Ollard and other judicious persons regard the publication of the *Remains* as a blunder which simply excited antagonism and caused the Oxford

Movement to be falsely regarded as pro-Roman, and one immediate effect, indeed, was the erection by public subscription of what is known in Oxford as the Martyrs' Memorial to Cranmer, Ridley and Latimer.

In 1839 Newman began to have doubts about the English Church, and he became still more disturbed when the Church joined with the German Lutherans in the appointment of a sort of joint bishop in Jerusalem. He spent more and more of his time at Littlemore and less and less at Oxford, and if it might be, to still the doubts, ever growing more disturbing, he wrote Tract Number 90, which was published in the spring of 1841.

All through his life Stanley was fond of travel, and in the year 1841 he was a great deal on the Continent, describing his impressions in long and singularly attractive letters. He was intensely moved by natural beauty and he was a keen and original observer, and the letters are full of such striking statements as his description of Palermo: 'The scenery is exactly what Sicilian scenery should be – a Greek plain surrounded by Italian hills.' Very acute, too, is the letter written from Rome in Holy Week: 'If I were already inclined to Roman Catholicism, they (the Easter ceremonies) would tend to make me a Papist; once granting that the general thing is desirable, they most forcibly impress one with the great convenience of having one man and one city and one Church which shall be able to play with the utmost possible solemnity the chief part of this great religious service.' Stanley evidently found a non-papal Catholicism unthinkable.

He returned from this Roman trip to Oxford in time for the excitement of Tract Number 90, the object of which was to show 'how patient the articles are of a Catholic interpretation on certain points where they have been usually taken to pronounce the unqualified condemnation of Catholic doctrine and opinions or to maintain Protestant ones.' Newman's attempt was certainly magnificent. The Articles had always been regarded, not unnaturally, as a bulwark of Protestantism, and the suggestion that they were really Catholic, as it were without knowing it, was sufficiently startling. 'When I first read Number 90,' declared an Evangelical leader, 'I did not know the author, but I said then and I repeat here, not with any personal reference to the author, that I should be sorry to trust the author of that Tract with my purse.' The Tract was published on February 27, and on March 8 four tutors, among whom was Tait of Balliol, afterwards Archbishop of Canterbury and father-in-law of the present Archbishop, made a formal protest, and the Heads of Houses, without permitting Newman to make any explanation, condemned the Tract, and ordered the condemnation to be posted in the college buttery hatches and at the gates of the schools.

The Heads of the Oxford colleges eighty years ago were a body of narrow-minded autocrats, living in what Dean Church called 'sublime and imbecile security,' apathetic, out of touch with life, generally dull and often vulgar, as when one of them, having received a letter from a Tractarian with the heading 'St. Luke's Day,' headed his reply 'Washing Day.' Of them all in 1841, two only, Dr. Routh, the President of Magdalen, and Dr. Richards, the Rector of Exeter, had any sort of comprehension of the significance of the Tractarian Movement or the smallest desire to be sympathetic or even judicious.

The Bishop of Oxford intervened after the condemnation of Newman and, while expressing his own disapproval of the steps that the Heads of Houses had taken, asked that the Tracts should be discontinued, and Newman at once agreed. Number 90 was the last of the series and it brought the history of the Tractarian movement proper to an end.

Tait had written long letters to Stanley telling him what had happened, and gleefully noting that Tractarianism had been proclaimed from one end of the kingdom to the other by the mouth of its own prophet to be twin sister of Popery. Stanley replied from his own peculiar point of view. He could not understand the excitement. He was astonished on his return home to find that Ward had resigned his Lectureships at Balliol, just as he was puzzled that Tait, another of his friends, should have compelled Ward's decision. And he was glad to escape for a while to London, where he met Wordsworth at the poet-banker Roger's famous breakfasts and for a while forgot theological controversy. His own position at this time is summarized in one of his letters: 'Faith founded the Church; hope has sustained it. I cannot help thinking that it is reserved for love to reform it.' If this means anything, it suggests that in the course of the ages faith had become of less moment than it had been at the beginning, an almost grotesque exaggeration of Latitudinarianism.

Arnold, who had left Rugby to become Professor of Modern History at Oxford in 1841, died of angina pectoris in the summer of 1842, and his death caused Stanley the bitterest personal sorrow. 'If he was not an apostle to others,' he said in one of his letters, 'he was an apostle to me,' and without delay he began the writing of his life of Arnold, which was published in 1844. As soon as he had finished his book, Stanley again went on a foreign tour, and among the notable and self-revealing expressions that I find in his letters is the statement that Berlin is a place which no Protestant should fail to visit, though the only reason I can conceive for any person ever going to Berlin would be to discover the horror of Protestantism.

The storm that had been aroused by the publication of Tract Number 90 had died down for a while, but only to be renewed. In 1843 Newman resigned the living of St. Mary's. In May of this year, Pusey preached before the University on 'the Holy Eucharist the Comfort to the Penitent,' and was at once accused of heresy, tried in his absence by six doctors of divinity and condemned for teaching doctrine contrary to the Church of England and ordered not to preach again in the University for two years. His judges were his notorious opponents, and an obviously unfair sentence aroused a storm of lay protest in which Mr. Gladstone took a leading part. In the long vacation of 1844, W. G. Ward published his *The Ideal of a Christian Church*. It is not a very wise book, and indeed in many respects is notably muddle-headed, and it supplied just the occasion that the anti-Tractarians wanted. Dr. Symons, Warden of Wadham, 'a violent man,' as Canon Ollard calls him, was Vice-Chancellor, and steps were taken to censure Ward, to degrade him from his degrees, and at the same time, in order to kill two birds with one stone, formally to condemn Tract Number 90 which, it will be remembered, had been published four years before. Ward was a master of indiscretion. Mr. Lytton Strachey has described him as 'a young man who had an extraordinary aptitude for *a priori* reasoning with a passionate devotion to *opéra bouffe.*' Stanley said of him: —

'He is very uncouth in appearance, as you know, and also uncouth in his tastes; at least, he has no taste for beauty of scenery, and not much for beauty of poetry. On the other hand, he is passionately fond of music, and I should think that his taste in that line is very good. On these points, therefore, we have not much in common. But what I do like very much in him is his great honesty, and fearless and intense love of truth, and his deep interest in all that concerns the happiness of the human race. These I never saw so strongly developed in anybody. We first became acquainted from his expressing, in my presence, his great admiration of Arnold, merely from a knowledge of his writings; and this, not having been diminished by our further intercourse, has, of course, proved a great point of union. He is the best arguer and the most clear-headed man that I ever saw; though, in one way, his logical faculty is one of his defects, for it has attained such gigantic heights as rather to overshadow some of the other parts of his mind. He is also enthusiastically fond of mathematics, and, I believe, a very good mathematician. He is very fond of me, and, added to these points, he is a very good man, very humble, very devout, very affectionate, and has done a great deal to improve himself since I knew him. He has been badly educated, and therefore, though very well informed on many points, is on many others, such as modern history and geography, excessively ignorant. I have said so much about him because I am afraid that, from what you have

171

seen of him, you might very naturally, but very seriously, underrate him. Almost all his worst points, his shyness, awkwardness, love of arguing, and want of love for physical beauty, come out at first very often, and give people an erroneous impression.'

Convocation met in a snow-storm on February 13, 1845. Ward defended himself with great humour, but his book was condemned and he was degraded from his degrees by considerable majorities. When the Convocation proceeded to discuss the condemnation of Tract 90, the Proctors, one of whom was Church, vetoed the proposal. Stanley was against the dominant party on all three issues, and his customary advocacy of all-round toleration is expressed in a memorandum that he published three days before Convocation met: —

'1. In 1836, Dr. Hampden was censured by Convocation on an undefined charge of want of confidence. In 1845, Mr. Newman and Mr. Ward are to be censured by the same body.

'2. In 1836, the country was panic-stricken with a fear of Liberalism. In 1845, the country is panic-stricken with a fear of Popery.

'3. 474 was the majority that condemned Dr. Hampden; 474 is the number of requisitionists that induced the censure on Mr. Newman.

'4. The censure on Dr. Hampden was brought forward at ten days' notice. The censure on Mr. Newman was brought forward at ten days' notice.

'5. Two Proctors of decided character, and of supposed leaning to the side of Dr. Hampden, filled the Proctor's office in 1836. Two Proctors of decided character, and of supposed leaning to the side of Mr. Newman, fill the Proctor's office in 1845.

'6. The *Standard* newspaper headed the attack on Dr. Hampden. The *Standard* newspaper heads the attack on Mr. Ward and Mr. Newman.

'7. The *Globe* and *Morning Chronicle* defended Dr. Hampden. The *Globe* and *Morning Chronicle* defend Mr. Ward.

'8. The Thirty-nine Articles were elaborately contrasted with the writings of Dr. Hampden as the ground of his condemnation. The Thirty-nine Articles are made the ground of the condemnation of Mr. Ward and Mr. Newman.

'9. The "Bampton Lectures" were preached four years before they were censured. The 90th *Tract for the Times* was written four years before it is now proposed to be censured.

'10. Two eminent lawyers pronounced the censure on Dr. Hampden illegal. Two eminent lawyers pronounce the degradation of Mr. Ward illegal.

'The wheel is come full circle round. The victors of 1836 are the victims of 1845. The victims of 1836 are the victors of 1845. The assailants are the assailed, the assailed are the assailants. The condemned are the condemners, the condemners the condemned.

'The wheel is come full circle round. How soon may it come round again; Voters of the 13th, deal to your opponents that justice which, perhaps, you may not expect to receive from them. But the truest hope of obtaining mercy or justice then is by showing mercy and justice now. Judge, therefore, by 1836 what should be your conduct in 1845, what should be your opponents' conduct in 1856, when Puseyism may be as triumphant as it is now depressed, when none can with any face protest against a mob tribunal then, if they have appealed to it now, or deprecate the madness of a popular clamour then, if they have kindled or added to it now.'

Stanley himself attended the meeting in the Sheldonian Theatre with Jowett, an old intimate Balliol friend. He commented on the proceedings as follows: --

'The more I reflect upon it, the more simply shocking is the impression left. A mob of 1,200 persons assuming judicial functions, after the most solemn warnings of their incompetency, on a question which it is quite impossible they can have studied, and then proceeding to inflict a sentence such as, in its present form, has never been inflicted on anyone in the whole history of the University. . . . The great mass, I suppose, voted on both sides with their party, the Puseyite side voting for Ward, as they would vote against Whately, or had voted against Hampden; the others, as they had voted, and will vote, against anyone who breaks in on the established usage. . . . "What are you going to do?" one old clergyman was heard to say to another. "Oh, I do not know -- vote for the old Church, I suppose; come and have a rubber afterwards." The Doctors gave their votes as they sat aloft in the semicircle. A flush, it is said, passed over the pallid face of the Provost of Oriel as he voted for the degradation; the others filed out at the two doors by each of which stood one of the two Proctors. It must have been a trying thing for Church, the Junior Proctor, friend of Newman and Ward, to see the tide rolling by, his blood boiling, as he said, from time to time, as, one after the other, men,

174

notorious for utter worldliness, gave their "placets" for the degradation.'

There was a curiously large undergraduate sympathy with Ward and a still more wide resentment at the attempt to prosecute Newman, and it was therefore wisely decided not to proceed any further against Tract Number 90. Newman did not attend the Convocation and remained silent till the autumn, when he resigned his Fellowship of Oriel, and on October 9 he was received into the Roman Catholic Church. 'This,' wrote Stanley, 'is a melancholy fact of which the ultimate consequences are incalculable.' Newman's example was not followed, as it had been hoped and feared. Keble, Pusey and Church remained within the fold of the English Church. Pusey, indeed, began again to preach before the University in 1846, and the subject of his first sermon was 'Absolution.' His attitude and point of view had been entirely unaffected by Newman's recession. Stanley never cared for Pusey's preaching and he said of the sermon that 'it was like most of his sermons, a divine soul clothed in a very earthly body.'

With all the theological excitement of the time, Stanley was living at Oxford the pleasant scholarly life of a Don, caring for his pupils, preaching an occasional sermon, intelligently interested in public affairs. As a theologian, he resented the limitation imposed upon him by Oxford orthodoxy, and, remembering how intimately he was to be connected with the Prince Consort, who was largely responsible for popularizing German heresy in England, there is considerable significance in his biographer's remark that in 1846 Stanley was 'forced to seek in German thought that mental freedom which had been

banished from Oxford.' With all his tolerance, and there
is no doubt that it was both frank and genuine, Stanley
had not the slightest idea of the qualities of men who
fervently held to an undiluted faith. This is shown with
almost comic completeness in his often-quoted remark:
'How different might have been the course of the Church
of England if Newman had been able to read German!'
Pusey could certainly read German and he was entirely
unaffected by German rationalism!

At this time, as always, Stanley was the earnest defender of the Establishment. His Church was the National
Church, and not the Catholic Church. He almost rejoiced
in its subjection to the Judicial Committee of the Privy
Council. He was all for comprehensiveness, for the inclusion of both Protestants and Catholics so long as the
Protestants were not too Protestant and the Catholics not
too Catholic. After the conversion – or perversion – of
Newman, there was a period of comparative calm until
1850, when the Bishop of Exeter declined to institute
a certain Mr. Gorham to a benefice because of that
clergyman's alleged denial of the doctrine of Baptismal
regeneration. Proceedings followed, and the Judicial
Committee finally decided that Mr. Gorham's views were
'not contrary or repugnant to the doctrine of the Church
of England as by law established.' The judgment has an
historical interest since it took Manning into the Church
of Rome. Incidentally it should not be forgotten that, to
quote Mr. Lytton Strachey, 'The judgment still holds
good; and to this day a clergyman of the Church of
England is quite at liberty to believe that regeneration
does not inevitably take place when an infant is baptized.'
Stanley was naturally on Gorham's side. He defended him

and attacked the Bishop of Exeter in an article in the *Edinburgh Review*, contending that a diocesan had no right to impose a new test on his clergy.

Stanley's father died in 1849. 'The crash, the gloom, the up-rooting and the void,' he wrote, 'are at times overwhelming.' Soon afterwards he refused the Deanery of Carlisle, preferring to stay on at Oxford where he was now busy with University reform, having been appointed secretary of a Commission of which Tait was one of the members. The Commission, which he considerably influenced, reported in 1852, and the result was the Act of 1854 which modernized the government and the scholastic life of the University. In 1851, before the Commission reported, Stanley accepted a canonry of Canterbury. He left Oxford with great regret, but he felt it his duty to make a home for his widowed mother and his one unmarried sister, and it was not without some relief that he escaped from ecclesiastical wranglings.

He was away from England on another of his tours in southern Europe in the autumn of 1852, returning home in time for the funeral of the Duke of Wellington, and in his account of the proceedings there is one of the self-illuminative passages that so constantly occur in his letters. He wrote: 'To me there was something awfully impressive in the mere Protestantism of the service: grand hopes of immortality, deep sense of irreparable loss, exhortations to duty, but not a word of prayer or thought, or wish for the dead himself. My reason acquiesced in the omission, but what an abnegation of natural human feeling! What a courage in the reformers who swept it away.'

I do not profess to understand admiration for the courage of persons, so blind to the significance of the Christian religion, as to make an entirely unnecessary abnegation of natural human feeling. The rejection by the sixteenth century reformers of Prayers for the Dead is something beyond my comprehension, with its implied limitation of the power of God, and its indifference to the fate of the departed, without, that is, the acceptance of the crude and cruel creed that was preached by Calvin to the unfortunate people of Geneva and which Stanley and the nineteenth century Latitudinarians certainly did not hold.

During the Crimean war Stanley's sister, who died a Roman Catholic, went out as a nurse to the Crimea to suffer not a little at the hands of 'the rabid Protestant party.' 'On one occasion,' Stanley reports, 'she was sternly reprimanded by a chaplain for giving a book of a very improper tendency to a wounded midshipman.'

In 1856 Tait was appointed Bishop of London and Stanley was offered and accepted the Professorship of Ecclesiastical History at Oxford with the Canonry of Christ Church which is attached to the Professorship. Stanley returned to Oxford, a man of forty-six, with assured position and considerable reputation as a scholar and divine. His published books included *Sinai and Palestine*, which he wrote after a visit to the Holy Land and which Pusey denounced for its careful omission of any reference to miracles; *The Epistles of St. Paul to the Corinthians*, which was a companion work to Jowett's *Commentary on the Epistles to the Thessalonians, Galatians and Romans*, and his *Historical Memorials of Canterbury*, in which he tells the story of the death of Becket with great dramatic power. In 1857 he continued his exploration of foreign lands with a journey to Russia and Sweden. He was dazzled by the beauty of the vestments used in the Swedish churches, apparently not realizing that this curious Lutheran institution possessed the outward trappings and little of the reality of sacramental religion.

Stanley had much enjoyed his life at Canterbury, but he was glad to be back in Oxford and again to be in touch with young opinion, though the signs of the times did not bring comfort or joy to his liberal heart. 'This generation,' he wrote, 'is either plunged in dogmatism or agnosticism. I look forward to the generation which is to come.' It is difficult to determine of whom Stanley most disapproved, the dogmatist or the agnostic. Among the men who attended his lectures was John Richard Green, who wrote to him years afterwards: 'I used to think as I left your lecture room of how many different faiths and persons you had spoken and how you had revealed and taught me to love the good that was in them all. I cannot tell you how that great principle of fairness has helped ever since; how in my reading it has helped me out of partisanship and mere hero worship.'

In 1860 the Church was again disturbed, this time by the publication of *Essays and Reviews*. Among the seven writers were Temple, at that time Head Master of Rugby, afterwards Bishop of London and Archbishop of Canterbury and the father of the Bishop of Manchester; Jowett of Balliol, and Mark Pattison, who had reacted from the influence of Newman to a very advanced Liberalism. Stanley was invited to contribute to the volume, but he declined, regarding the whole scheme as a decided blunder. The essays are of unequal merit and the publication was, as it was obviously intended to be, extremely provocative. Stanley was always for peace. He held firmly to his opinions, but he preferred to whisper them in a study rather than to shout them on a house-top. But when the book was attacked, and particularly when, as he thought, his friends Temple and Jowett were misrepresented, he hastened to their aid. Bishop Wilberforce, whose sympathies with the Tractarians were well known, wrote a severe criticism of *Essays and Reviews* in the *Quarterly*, and Stanley published a reply in the *Edinburgh*. The book was condemned by the Bishops in 1861, and Stanley at once challenged their action in a letter that he addressed to Tait. He suggested that his friends had been condemned without a proper consideration of their writing, and, according to his policy of toleration, he contended that there was room for all the seven writers within the wide and expansive bosom of the National Church, which needed the 'learning of the most learned, the freedom of the freed, the reason of the most rational.' *Essays and Reviews* was condemned by the Lower House of Convocation of the province which Temple was one day to rule, and it was expected for a time that he would be forced to resign his head mastership of Rugby.

Stanley's writing in the *Edinburgh* brought him into considerable trouble with more than one bishop. But he was satisfied when his beloved Judicial Committee of the Privy Council, in a majority judgment with which the Archbishops disapproved, justified the Essays and specifically declared that the Church of England does not hold the doctrines of Verbal Inspiration, Imputed Righteousness and Eternal Punishment.

In 1860 Stanley delivered his lectures on the Eastern Church, the materials for which he had carefully collected in Greece and Russia. In 1861 he made another long tour through eastern Europe.

Thanks probably to his well-known sympathy with German Liberal theology, Stanley had been appointed one of the chaplains of the Prince Consort, but he does not appear to have been very much in touch with the Court until after the death of the Prince in 1861, which moved him to the amazing remark: 'So long as he lived I felt sure he was a steady support to all that was most excellent in the English Church. That barrier is now thrown down and through the chasm, God protect us from the spirits that will rush in!' Strange indeed was it for a divine who cherished the existence of a Church that was above all things national, to fear that Church's disappearance unless it were protected by a foreign prince whose religion was definitely German and not English, and who never for one moment showed any appreciation of the peculiar character of the Church of Andrewes and of Laud.

Three weeks after the Prince Consort's funeral, Stanley learned from General Bruce, the Queen's private secretary, that it had been the Prince's wish that he should accompany the Prince of Wales on a journey to the Holy Land. Stanley agreed with reluctance and misgiving, particularly because his mother was in a delicate state of health, and he spent the first six months of 1862 in an interesting and extended journey through Egypt and the Holy Land. His mother actually died on Ash Wednesday, and Stanley, whose deep family affection was one of the most appealing of his qualities, was heart-broken. 'Every morning,' he wrote, 'I wake with a tearful recollection of that sweet face and dear voice.' But he determined to go on, rather quaintly saying in a letter to Jowett: 'It is a melancholy satisfaction to me that through this accidental link of my journey with the Prince, her death has assumed something of a national character.' The vanity is pathetic, but the genuineness of his sorrow found beautiful expression again in a letter to Jowett: 'Nothing that has happened, nothing I trust that can happen, can make her memory other than the greatest gift I have received.'

General Bruce, who had been one of the Prince's suite in the Palestine journey and had become very intimate with Stanley, died soon after their return to London, and a common sorrow was the beginning of an intimate friendship with Bruce's sisters which was to have a considerable effect on his future life.

Stanley was concerned in one more bitter ecclesiastical wrangle before his Oxford career came to a final end. In 1861 and 1862, Colenso, a mathematician and incidentally Bishop of Natal, published critical volumes on the Pauline Epistles and the Pentateuch. Stanley did not disagree with the Bishop's opinions, but as before he deprecated the publication of Liberal theological volumes calculated to stir up strife. In a letter to Colenso he said: 'My object for twenty years and my object in my forthcoming book, is to draw forth the inestimable treasures of the Old Testament both historically, geographically, morally and spiritually. To fix the public attention on the mere defects of structure and detail is, to my mind, to lead off the public mind on a false scent and to a false issue.' And he urged the Bishop to consider the wisdom of the advice, 'Be not martyrs by mistake.'

In 1863 Stanley published his letter on 'The State of Subscription in the Church of England and in the University of Oxford,' protesting against the pledges which the University demanded of its members and urging that a relaxation would stem 'the gradual falling off in the supply of the intelligent, thoughtful, and highly educated young men who twenty and thirty years ago were to be found at every ordination.' Two years later Parliament passed an Act which Convocation ratified modifying the traditional assent, but the idea that men can be attracted to a Church by asking them to believe as little as possible, though it is still fondly held by the Modernists, has always proved an entire and a grotesque illusion. Queen Victoria asked to read Stanley's letter and expressed her approval. Indeed, she was so pleased that she wanted to make the author a bishop, but Palmerston, for some reason or the other, would have none of him. However, he was constantly summoned to Windsor or to Osborne. He was always present at the Queen's lugubrious celebrations of the anniversary of her husband's death, and preached sermons much to the royal lady's taste. In 1863 Stanley went specially to Sandringham to administer the Sacrament to the Prince and Princess of Wales, going through the Service with the Princess on Easter Eve and explaining its differences from the Danish rite.

Stanley was growing weary of Oxford and of never-ceasing strife – in 1862 there was an attempt in which Pusey was concerned to prosecute Jowett for heresy; in 1863 Pusey was responsible for resisting the proposal to confer an honorary degree on Charles Kingsley on the extremely futile ground that *Hypatia* was not a fit book to be read by 'our wives and sisters,' – and when the Deanery of Westminster was offered to him in the autumn of the latter year, he promptly accepted it. Two days before he received Palmerston's letter, he announced his engagement to Lady Augusta Bruce, the sister of General Bruce, with whom Queen Victoria was more intimate than with any of her ladies. The Queen was anything but pleased, and she wrote caustically to her uncle: —

'You will be sorry to hear of two things — first, that I fear the King of P(russia) is again molesting poor Fritz, and secondly, that my dear Lady Augusta, at 41, without a previous long attachment, has, most unnecessarily, decided to *marry* (!!) that certainly *most* distinguished and excellent man, Dr. Stanley!! It has been my *greatest sorrow* and trial *since* my misfortune! I thought she *never* would leave *me*! She seems, however, to think that she can by *his* guidance be of more use than before even. She will remain in my service and be often with me, but it cannot be the *same*, for her first duty is *now* to another!'

In the recently published *Letters of Lady Augusta Stanley*, her nephew, the Dean of Windsor, has printed a delightful letter from her sister-in-law which suggests that the fear of the Queen must have considerably complicated the Dean's courtship of a very shy lady, a little troubled by his unorthodoxy, even though she attributed it to 'the straining of his loving heart to embrace and hold fast all and his immense power of seeing and understanding the difficulties of others.' Mrs. Bruce wrote: —

'The Queen must be told nothing more till the event is settled and the day named. H.M. dislikes courtship, was much bored with her daughters, during that time, even in happy days, and last year the P. of W. was kept abroad till Prs. Alexdra. had left Windsor. On no account must she see Dr. S. and A. under similar circumstances, and for Augusta's sake (who will be nervous and unsettled till all is arranged) I implore the Canon to act with decision and rapidity. People wd. never marry at all if they took so long to consider about it. They suit each other perfectly, know each other thoroughly, and being both of mature years, shd. lose no more time. I am very glad to hear he will not take Dublin. I do not fancy him there at all. At any rate I hope to see him in town.'

Without delay Stanley attempted to make the Abbey as comprehensive as he wished the Church to be, and in very warm and appreciative letters he invited Keble, Pusey and Liddon to preach at special Sunday evening services. They all refused. Keble wrote: 'Were I to accept it would be in discomfort and fear, lest by seeming to bear with doctrines which you avowedly uphold, and which I believe in my heart to contradict the foundation of the faith, I should cause harm which would far outweigh any good one might hope to do by preaching.' Pusey said: 'I believe the present to be a struggle for the life or death of the English Church, and what you believe to be for life, I believe to be for death.' And in a subsequent letter he said: 'I think that one of the great dangers of the present day is to conceive of matters of faith as if they were matters of opinion, to think all have an equal chance of being right which involves this — that there is no faith at all.' Liddon protested that 'on the most sacred questions we are hopelessly divided.'

The Tractarians, unlike some of their Anglo-Catholic successors, were not prepared to subscribe to the glorious gospel of comprehensiveness. Believing that the Church of England was the Church Catholic, they were unable to regard the yoking with Protestants and half-believers as anything more than a temporary trial to be brought to an end when the Church as a whole realized its character, its heritage, and its privileges. Liddon wrote to Stanley: 'A legal (rather than a moral) bond retains us within the same communion – or, rather, God's providence does so, I hope, and pray with a view to future unity of conviction, however that may seem at present.' It was the dream of the Tractarians that a little leaven would leaven the whole lump. They were fearful and perhaps intolerant of Liberal theology imported from Germany, but it was the conversion of the Protestant for which they prayed, and they never brought a railing accusation against the pious men who were often their eager persecutors. It was the Arnolds and the Kingsleys who railed, not the Kebles and the Liddons.

In his desire for complete comprehensiveness, Stanley was almost alone in his own day. Arnold would have welcomed Unitarians, but he would have drummed out the Tractarians. But since his death, the spirit of Stanley has conquered. His is the policy of the majority of the present episcopate. It is enshrined in the Composite Prayer Book. 'Let everybody be artistic in his own way. That's my motto as an upholsterer,' says a character in one of Mr. Henry Arthur Jones's comedies. 'Let everybody be religious in his own way,' is, thanks largely to Stanley, now the motto of the dominant party in the Church of England, though the proviso is added, 'so long as his religion is moderate and sane and so long as he does not believe anything over much.'

The Queen, who apparently soon forgave Stanley for taking away her favourite lady, shared his Liberalism. She warmly approved Stanley's defence of Colenso. She drew up a list of clergymen whom she recommended for preferment and included Stopford Brooke and Llewellyn Davies. If she had had her way, Stopford Brooke, who proclaimed himself a Unitarian in 1880, would have been a bishop in 1875. But the Queen had a horror of extremists of all sorts, of, as she told Disraeli, 'either Ritualists or people belonging to the Evangelical school, than whom no more narrow-minded or uncharitable people exist. Beware of such, they will drive people to Atheism or Catholicism.' But though she disliked the fervour of the Evangelical, it was the Ritualist whom the Queen abhorred. It was perhaps well for Stanley that Keble and Pusey and Liddon refused the invitation to preach in the Abbey, for their presence in his pulpit would certainly have gravely offended his mistress. She never forgave Wilberforce for his friendship with the Tractarians. After his death, she wrote: 'Many entertained grave doubts as to his conduct and views as a Churchman, which she must own was her own case.' She warned Gladstone that he was suspected of having 'rather a leaning to High Church views.' And it was the Queen more than any other single person who was responsible for the Public Worship Act. Indeed she compelled Disraeli, who really cared for none of these things, to force the Act through Parliament. The story begins with a letter that the Queen wrote to Stanley in 1873 in which she said: —

'The Queen *now* turns with much anxiety to the *very* pressing question of the *state* of the *English* Church; its Romanizing tendencies which she fears are on the increase, its relations with other Protestant Churches, and the *universal struggle*, which has begun between the Roman Catholic Church and Protestant Governments in general. She is sure that the Dean has heard and seen much in Italy which will throw light on this last. But as regards the English Church, which she perceives is being greatly threatened with disestablishment, action seems becoming necessary. This disestablishment the Queen would regret. She thinks a *complete Reformation* is what we want. But if *that* is *impossible*, the Archbishop should have the *power* given him, by *Parliament*, to *stop all* these Ritualistic practices, dressings, bowings, etc., and everything of that kind, and, *above all*, *all* attempts at *confession*. As the Ecclesiastical Courts can afford no *assistance* on this head, let the Bishops ask for power to put a stop to all these *new* and *very* dangerous as well as absurd practices, and at the same time, give permission to other Protestant Ministers to preach in our churches, and where there is no other church to perform their different services in the same, as is always *done* abroad.

'The Queen states all these points very crudely to the Dean, as her mind is greatly occupied with the state of the Church in England, and with the terrible amount of *bigotry* and *self-sufficiency* and *contempt* of all *other Protestant Churches*, of which she had some *incredible* instances the other day. The English Church should bethink itself of its dangers from *Papacy*, instead of trying to widen the breach with *all* other Protestant Churches, and to magnify small differences of form. The English Church should stretch out its arms to other Protestant Churches. The Queen has the greatest confidence in the Dean's courage and energy and wishes he could inspire the Archbishop and others with the same. For the time is coming, if not come, when *something will have* to be done, or – the Church will *fall*.'

The truth is that the Queen's religion, which with her politics she had acquired from her husband, was German Lutheranism. She disliked the character of the Church of England, however partially she understood it, and the Established Church of Scotland was her spiritual home. She was perfectly furious when, in 1866, Archbishop Longley went to Scotland to stimulate the Episcopal Church. She wrote to Dean Wellesley of Windsor, her constant adviser in all ecclesiastical affairs: –

'If it had been *merely* the Episcopalian Church of Scotland, as they are dissenters in Scotland, Dr. Macleod said it would *not* have signified; but when the Archbishop of Canterbury himself came to Scotland, and permits the Bishops to speak of "*the* Church" – implying, as they do, that the *Scotch* establishment is *no* Church, and her Sacraments not to be considered as such, which they openly do – the case becomes *very grave*. Now the Queen takes a solemn engagement, on her accession, to maintain the Established Church of Scotland, and any attempt to subvert it is *contrary* to Law, and indeed subversive of that respect for *existing Institutions* which, above all, the Archbishops and Bishops *ought* to do *everything* to maintain; and she *will* maintain it.

'But, quite apart from this, the Queen considers this movement as *most* mischievous. The Presbyterian Church is essentially *Protestant*, and, as such, *most* valuable. The Reformation in this country was *never* fully completed, and had we applied the pruning knife more severely, we should *never* have been exposed to the dangers to which the Church of England is *now* exposed, and for which the Queen thinks it will be *absolutely* necessary to take some measures.

'The Queen feels, *more strongly* than words *can* express, the duty which is imposed upon her and her family, to maint~in the *true* and *real principles* and *spirit* of the *Protestant* religion; for her family was brought over and placed on the throne of these realms *solely* to maintain it; and the Queen will *not* stand the attempts made to destroy the simple and truly Protestant faith of the Church of Scotland, and to bring the Church of England as near the Church of Rome as they possibly can.'

The Queen's dislike of Ritualism had probably been stimulated by the Bennett judgment of 1872. The Church Association had initiated the prosecution of the Rev. W. J. E. Bennett, vicar of Frome Selwood and a prominent member of the second generation of the Tractarians, for teaching the doctrine of the Real Objective Presence in the Holy Eucharist, and the Judicial Committee considering the case, as Stanley said, 'not in the heated atmosphere of partisan theologians but in the dry daylight of English law,' decided that such teaching was permissible within the English Church. The verdict was acclaimed as a victory for Anglo-Catholicism, but to Stanley it was 'the last crowning triumph of the Christian latitudinarianism of the Church of England.' Let everybody believe and teach what he likes! Six years earlier Stanley had defended Ritualistic practices in a debate in Convocation from his own peculiar and rather patronizing point of view. In the course of his speech he said:—

'Two nations or parties (as it was said a long time ago) were struggling in the womb of the Church of England, each one from time to time attempting to cast out the other. Neither has ever entirely succeeded, and I trust never will succeed to the end of time. That is one reason why these practices, if it is possible without rending asunder the practical unity of the Church, ought to be tolerated. Another reason why we should leave them without further notice is that . . . (except in the two aspects to which I have alluded — their defiance of the people and the bishops) they are innocent; that is, they have no malignant object. Many may think these practices foolish, but their greatest enemy will not say they have any object beyond that of aiding the devotions of the people, or of assimilating our services to the Churches of other communions. But those objects are not sinful; they do not tend to the engendering of evil passions; they are not of the nature of many of those pursuits in which so many of the clergy during the last few years have been engaged — attacking and excluding one excellent person after another, and promoting ill-will and misunderstanding between man and man. They only assume that character when adopted in antagonism to the bishops or the parishes. In themselves they are innocent — even their enemies being judges — and this is a sound reason why they should be permitted, if it can be done without the disruption of particular parishes, or disturbing the unity of the whole Church. . . .

'It is said that they symbolize important doctrines, which accounts for the great fight made for them; but that also accounts for the great fight made against them. It is my wish to show that there is no reason for the fight, either for them or against them. If we take the chief point in dispute, the "vestments," it is important once for all to remember what is their origin, and what doctrines or things they do or do not symbolize. An explanation has

191

been given of their origin – that they have grown out of the garments worn by the Apostles. But what were the garments of the Apostles, except just the common dress worn by the country-people at that time? These vestments, which have made so much noise, altered, of course, in the ages which have since elapsed, were neither more nor less than the shirt, the coat, and the overcoat of the Greek or Roman peasants of the time. When the tunicle, the alb, and the chasuble are adopted as an imitation of the Roman Catholic custom, that is another matter; but this is not the ground taken up. . . .

'This, then, is what I have to say on the matter – that these parties ought to be tolerated on the general principles by which the Church of England tolerates all that it can include within its pale; they ought to be tolerated because they are innocent; they ought to be let alone because they are "inapt," unsuitable to express any principle for or against which anyone is contending. Things which quicken one man's devotion do not affect another. With one it is Gothic, and with another Grecian, architecture. With some it is dresses like these, with some a white surplice, with others no surplice at all. All these things ought to be tolerated as so many helps to the devotion of the Church, according to the different ways in which they strike different minds. The only serious dangers are those to which I have before alluded, where they spread in defiance of the parish or the constituted authorities, or where they are exalted as if they made part of the essence of religion.'

While Gladstone was Prime Minister there was no chance of coercive anti-Anglo-Catholic legislation. But even before the formation of the Disraeli ministry of 1874, the Queen began to get busy. She opened her campaign with a letter to Tait, now become Archbishop of Canterbury. Something, she said, must be done to check 'the liberties taken and the defiance shown by the clergy of the High Church and Ritualistic party.' And sharing her predecessor Elizabeth's distrust of bishops, she suggested that there should be 'an admixture of laymen with the bishop to aid him in preventing these Romanizing practices.' Tait introduced the Public Worship Bill in the Lords and it was carried, but it was opposed by Gladstone in the Commons, and in the first division Disraeli was supported by only one of his Cabinet colleagues, Cross, the highly respectable solicitor whom, perhaps because of his Protestant fidelity, the Queen always held in high esteem. But Disraeli was eager to please the royal lady, 'Protestant to the very heart's core,' and with his usual address he contrived to persuade the Cabinet and even the most reluctant Lord Salisbury to give Government approval to the Bill. 'Mr. Disraeli,' wrote the delighted Queen, 'must have managed his refractory Cabinet most skilfully.' But the Queen was not satisfied until the Bill had actually passed. 'Pray show,' she wrote in another letter to Disraeli, 'that you are in earnest and determined to pass this Bill and not to be deterred by threats of delay.' And the Bill was carried. Disraeli professed to fear secessions from his ministry, but none occurred. No man preferred his religion to his place.

Stanley supported the Public Worship Act although he had always been opposed to such legislation. He and Tait had been so often in agreement that it would have been unpleasant to him to have resisted when the Archbishop so strenuously urged, and, moreover, his Erastianism would have made it difficult for him to have opposed the royal will. If he had been sincere in regarding the death of the Prince Consort as almost a fatal blow to the English Church, it would hardly have been possible for him to have been among the opponents of a policy which the Prince would have assuredly supported. Moreover, it probably seemed to him that the points of discipline which were in dispute were of no possible importance. What could it matter whether a clergyman celebrated the Holy Communion at the east side of the altar or at the north side?

Stanley's super-Erastianism was shown by his belittling of Convocation. As seen in the light of future Church development there is no little significance in his opinion that 'the only cure for Ritualism is the destruction of Convocation – *delenda est convocatio*.' For him Parliament and not the Provincial Synods was the supreme court of the Church of England, and if he had been logical – few men are – he would have regarded disestablishment as the death of the Church. In a debate in Convocation he said: –

'I was shocked and surprised the other day, in the House of Lords, to hear a right rev. prelate whom I greatly respect distinguish between his position as a peer of Parliament and his position as a Father in God, speaking as if he were only a peer of Parliament when Parliament was sitting, and only a Father in God when sitting in the Upper House of Convocation. I entirely repudiate any such distinction. I regard the Bishops of this realm as much more Fathers in God when they are sitting in the supreme council of the nation, addressing the peers of England, than when they are talking to half a dozen reporters in a private drawing-room in Dean's Yard. It is most desirable, at all events, that if there be anybody in this House who values the importance of maintaining the supremacy of law, and of protesting against those usurpations to which I have just alluded, they ought freely and openly to express their feelings on that subject, as their duty alike to the State and the Church, alike to the Imperial Legislature and to their brethren in this House.'

Before returning to the record of the Dean's remaining years, it is worth while to study in the valuable Victorian diary exactly how that State system which Stanley valued so highly actually worked. The Queen insisted on exercising the Crown patronage herself. She would listen to advice, but she nearly always contrived to have her own way. It was she, prompted certainly by Wellesley and probably by Stanley, who insisted that Tait should succeed Longley at Canterbury in 1868. Disraeli resisted so long as he dared. Tait was a Liberal in politics and in theology, and Disraeli was a profound believer in the principle of spoils for the victor, particularly just before a general election, when the victors would probably be vanquished. His nominee was Ellicott, Bishop of Gloucester, whom Wellesley scornfully described as a man with 'a miserably thin weak voice and no dignity of manner.' Disraeli's criticism of Tait is delicious. He wrote to the Queen: —

'Acknowledging his abilities and virtues, Mr. Disraeli finds him, as an Ecclesiastical statesman, obscure in purpose, fitful and inconsistent in action, and evidently, though earnest and conscientious, a prey to constantly conflicting convictions. It is true he behaved with courage on the question of the Colonial Bishops, but he favoured the Synod, the origin of all these embarrassments; and he is, at this moment, from some influence which Mr. Disraeli cannot trace, as much compromised with respect to religious sisterhoods, as the Bishops of Salisbury and Oxford themselves.

'This is to be observed of the Bishop of London, that, though apparently of a spirit somewhat austere, there is in his idiosyncrasy a strange fund of enthusiasm, a quality which ought never to be possessed by an Archbishop of Canterbury, or a Prime Minister of England. The Bishop of London sympathizes with everything that is earnest; but what is earnest is not always true; on the contrary, error is often more earnest than truth.'

It was natural that Disraeli should regard earnestness in an Archbishop as grotesque, but he had to give way. Gladstone was naturally inclined to take his Church patronage very seriously, and he certainly never sacrificed what seemed to him to be the good of the Church to mere party considerations. He claimed indeed that all the clergymen suggested by him for preferment were 'specially known as scholars, or as weighty writers and divines or for having rendered eminent service to education or as powerful preachers or very able and effective pastors.' Disraeli had no such scruples. He urged one appointment because it 'would gratify the Conservative party generally,' and another of his nominees had as a special qualification that he had been a friend of the Prime Minister's father. He warned the Queen that favour shown to the Broad Church party, which for some odd reason he particularly disliked, would disrupt the Cabinet. And the Queen sharply pointed out 'the immense danger to the Church which will inevitably fall, if men of intellect and enlightened views are excluded for fear of frightening members of the government and of Parliament.' But the royal favour itself was sometimes eccentric. A Mr. Birch was suggested because his preferment would please the Prince of Wales, in addition to which he and his wife desired to move to a healthier locality. Some years afterwards the Queen insisted that Duckworth should have the Westminster Canonry, vacant by the death of Kingsley. Duckworth had been governor to Prince Leopold, who at that time was very ill, and 'the appointment would greatly gratify her poor sick boy.' Stanley suggested that Bradley, then Master of University College, Oxford, and destined to be his successor, would be a better selection. He was indeed anxious that his Chapter should be strengthened. Church had been Dean of St. Paul's since 1871, and Liddon, who had accepted a canonry a year earlier, was drawing all London to St. Paul's by his sermons. And since Kingsley's death, Stanley's one colleague of the smallest distinction was 'Eric or Little by Little' Farrar. But Bradley was rejected and Duckworth was chosen, and the Queen wrote to Disraeli: 'He would have been gratified had he seen the pleasure which lighted up the emaciated face of the dear invalid.' So the State system worked and so it still works – one bishop ruled out for his thin voice, another criticized for too great earnestness, a canon chosen to humour a sick prince!

In 1870 Stanley was appointed a member of the Committee appointed by Convocation to revise the New Testament. Among the members of this Committee were certain Nonconformists, including the Unitarian Dr. Vance Smith. The first meeting of the Committee was preceded by a celebration of the Holy Eucharist in Henry VII's chapel in Westminster Abbey, and Stanley invited all its members, including the Unitarian, to make their Communion, a proceeding properly denounced as an act of blasphemy and 'a deliberate embodiment of insult and defiance to the whole of Catholic Christendom.' A vote of censure on Stanley was passed in the Upper House of Convocation, but after a long debate and after listening to an eloquent defence from Stanley, the Lower House refused to endorse the resolution of the bishops. The incident is of importance since it suggests the impassable gulf that lay between Stanley and the Tractarians in their antagonistic conceptions of the character and significance of the Holy Eucharist. And this he showed again when some years later he consented to give Communion to Mrs. Annie Besant, who professed herself an unbeliever but who wished to give a small measure of satisfaction to her dying mother, who refused to take the Communion unless her daughter shared it with her. Mrs. Besant quite naturally eulogized Stanley as 'that gentle noble heart,' but he was certainly guilty of an action which the greater part of Christendom would regard as blasphemy.

In 1872 Stanley was again troubled by the Athanasian Creed which was fated to be his King Charles's head. He was eager that the Creed should be omitted altogether from the Services of the English Church, and in a speech in Convocation he repeated his condemnation of the damnatory clauses. On the other side, Liddon and Pusey promptly declared that if the Creed was either mutilated or degraded they would be compelled to leave the Ministry of the Church, and in the Convocation debate Archdeacon Denison left the House rather than listen to Stanley's onslaught. One consequence was a demand that his name should be erased from the list of Oxford's select preachers. In the petition he was described, I think not unfairly, as 'the advocate of the Westminster sacrilegious Communion; the partisan of Mr. Voysey, the infidel; the avowed champion of a negative and cloudy Christianity which is really preparing the way for the rejection of all revealed truth.'

But Stanley was personally popular and the boycott was defeated, though only by a small majority. The outcome of the controversy was that by a compromise, and in spite of Stanley's opposition, Convocation solemnly declared that 'the confession of our Christian faith commonly called the Creed of St. Athanasius doth not make any addition to the faith as contained in Holy Scripture but warneth against errors which from time to time have arisen in the Christian Church.'

Pusey's feeling concerning the Athanasian Creed was shown in a letter that he addressed to Liddon just before a meeting called by the English Church Union: —

'Words dictated from a very sick bed must be very true. Yes. I wish to express, through you, to the Meeting, how unchanging, through sickness or health, is my sense of the intensity of the crisis with which we were threatened all last year, and out of which the Church of England has, by God's mercy, been brought. However men might disguise the question themselves, I could not conceal from myself that the real issue was, whether the Church of

England should virtually deny that the faith in the Holy Trinity, and in the Incarnation of our Lord Jesus Christ, was essential to salvation in those who could have it. As to the remarks of some in authority, as to the line to which our convictions independently led us, they cannot have understood the strength of our convictions. It was no "threat" to give up, in my case, the cherished aspirations of the past sixty years to serve God in the ministry of the Church of England, the home and centre of one's deepest interests – to go forth not knowing whither one went. It was like a moral death; but with my convictions of the issue of that question, I dared no more hesitate than about being guilty of parricide. God be thanked for all His mercies.'

As Dean of Westminster, Stanley spent a busy life, his activities including much literary work, among other things two books of lectures on the Jewish Church, *The Memorials of Westminster Abbey*, and many articles in the *Edinburgh Review*. He himself said that *The Memorials of Westminster Abbey* was 'not a good book,' and it certainly is not. It is, indeed, amazingly dull, and it never for one moment occurred to the author that one of the most beautiful buildings in the world was profaned and made comparatively ugly by the monuments to fools and knaves! In the Providence of God, it may happen one of these days that a Dean of Westminster will clear out all the rubbish and throw it into the Thames, and then a wonderful building erected for the worship of God and degraded into a cemetery for men – some of them none too reputable – will be returned to its original purpose.

Stanley was smug in his satisfaction with the 'illustrious

sepulchres' with which the Abbey is cumbered. It did not appear to him the least bit incongruous that unbelievers should be buried in a Christian church. He writes: 'Courayer, the foreign Latitudinarian, Ephraim Chambers, the sceptic of the humbler, and Sheffield, the sceptic of the higher ranks, were buried with all respect and honour by the 'College of Priests' at Westminster, who thus acknowledged that the bruised reed was not to be broken nor the smoking flax quenched.' This is high-sounding nonsense, the truth being that since the Reformation a complacent Dean has been frequently persuaded to permit the burial within the Abbey both of the sceptic and of the comparatively obscure. The inclusion, to quote Stanley's phrase, of 'the licentious Congreve' among the Abbey dead, was a disgraceful scandal. It appears, indeed, the more repulsive after reading Stanley's suave words: 'The godlike gift of genius was recognized, the baser earthly part was left to the merciful judgment of its creator.'

Stanley was always eager to point the moral and adorn the tale, and there is one delightful passage in *Memorials of Westminster Abbey* so characteristic as to be worth quoting at length: —

'And if our moral indignation is also aroused against the prominence of many a name now forgotten, yet the same mixture of mortification and satisfaction which is impressed upon us as we see, in the monuments, the proof of the fallibility of artistic judgment, is impressed upon us in a deeper sense as we read, in the history of their graves, or their epitaphs, a like fallibility of moral and literary judgment. In this way the obscure poets and warriors who have attained the places which we now so bitterly grudge them, teach us a lesson never to be despised. They tell us of the writings, the works, or the deeds in which our fathers delighted; they remind us that the tombs and the graves which now so absorb our minds may in like manner cease to attract our posterity; they put forward their successors to plead for their perpetuation, at least in the one place where alone, perhaps, a hundred years hence either will be remembered. And if a mournful feeling is left upon our minds by the thought that so many reputations, great in their day, have passed away; yet here and there the monuments contain the more reassuring record, that there are glories which increase instead of diminishing as time rolls on, and that there are judgments in art and in literature, as well as in character, which will never be reversed.'

To Stanley, the Abbey was a possession of the nation rather than of the Church itself, 'a sanctuary not of any private sect, but of the English people.' And apparently he meant by the phrase, 'a private sect,' the Church of which he was a priest. Indeed he labours the point that to him all Christians are members of the National Church, whether they like it or not. He says, 'It (the Abbey) is endeared both to the conforming and non-conforming members of the National Church.' Considering how widely Stanley's theories are now accepted, it is well to emphasize this peculiar point of view. The English Church, as he saw it, is not even a society of the baptized. He accepts the full Erastian contention that all subjects of the English king who profess any form of Christianity are necessarily and by right members of the English Church, whether they are confirmed or not; whether they believe the Creeds or not; whether they are Parthians or Medes or the dwellers in Mesopotamia.

Stanley, though still a professed Liberal, opposed the disestablishment of the Irish Church, and he evolved a plan for the settlement of the Irish religious troubles which was too elaborate for practical politicians. At Westminster he added to the monuments as if there were not enough already, restored the Chapter House, arranged week-day lectures by Nonconformists in the nave and celebrated Maundy Thursday with a performance of Bach's Passion Music, the trappings, that is, of the Passion story without the insistence on its reality. An Anglo-Catholic organ said: 'The church was crammed and the audience – congregation would be a misnomer – was very much the same as at any other concert.' And Stanley really thought that he was making a daring religious innovation!

After, as before his marriage, Stanley found time each year for a continental holiday. In 1866 he was again in Rome and was received by Pius IX who, gossiping with him about well-known English ecclesiastics, said: 'When you meet Pusey give him this message from me – that I compare him to a bell which always sounds to invite the faithful to church and itself remains outside.'

In 1869 Stanley was gratified by the appointment of Temple to the Bishopric of Exeter on the nomination of the High Church Gladstone, though the appointment was denounced by Pusey as 'the most frightful enormity that had ever been perpetrated by a Prime Minister.' One can only be glad that Dr. Pusey had gone to his eternal rest before Mr. Ramsay Macdonald appointed Dr. Barnes as Bishop of Birmingham, for one hesitates to think to what excessive expletive a kindly and pious man would have been compelled. Temple was consecrated in Westminster Abbey and, though protests were handed in to the Bishop of London, the expected brawling did not take place.

I have already referred to Stanley's connection with the Rev. Charles Voysey, who in his later years had an independent Unitarian chapel off Piccadilly. Voysey was a defiant zealot who disbelieved the assertions of the Christian Creeds and was eager to advertise his want of faith. Stanley did not quarrel with his opinions though he certainly considered that Voysey went a great deal too far, but as usual he deprecated all vociferous incidents that were certain to stir up trouble. Voysey was condemned, and very properly condemned, for heresy. The verdict was upheld by the Judicial Committee, and Stanley addressed to the eager heretic a letter which in polite terms practically said 'it serves you right.'

With more than one present-day Dean, Stanley was vastly interested in the Old Catholics, that most recent and, in many respects, pathetic break away from the Roman Church, which was recently described as so old as to be almost senile, and in 1872 he attended their congress in Cologne. In the 'seventies the most picturesque rebel against Rome was Père Hyacinthe who, after having found the most exalted reasons for his revolt against the Papacy, demonstrated its real reason by getting married, much to the discomfort of Stanley and his other admirers. As was said of him in France: — *Il a parlé de l'Infaillibilité et ce n'etait qu'un prétexte. Ce beau drame finit par une comédie.* Perhaps indeed Lutheranism itself would never have existed had Luther not yearned to marry a nun.

In 1874 Stanley went to St. Petersburg to celebrate the

Anglican marriage of the Duke of Edinburgh, Queen Victoria's second son, and the Grand Duchess Marie of Russia. Lady Augusta was entrusted by the Queen with a box containing two prayer books, 'the one in white with an illumination of some verses which I had painted on purpose is for the Grand Duchess and the other plain one is for Alfred.' Stanley enjoyed himself vastly in the Winter Palace at St. Petersburg, as it was then called, with its sixteen hundred rooms and four thousand inhabitants. The Russian revolution and all that it has meant to the outside world was far enough away in 1874.

It was on an Ash Wednesday that Stanley's mother died, and his wife died on Ash Wednesday, 1876. The two great sorrows of his life were commemorated in a poem which began: —

'O Day of Ashes! twice for me
    Thy mournful title hast thou earned,
For twice my life of life by thee
    Has been to dust and ashes turned.
No need, dark day, that thou shouldst borrow
    The trappings of a formal sorrow;
In thee are cherish'd, fresh and deep,
    Long memories that cannot sleep.'

Queen Victoria wrote in her Diary the day after Lady Augusta's death: —

'Before breakfast heard that my dearest friend Augusta was, alas! no more. She died quite peacefully last night. Too sad! But yet what a blessed release from such cruel sufferings! Sent Janie Ely up to the Deanery to ask for details. Walked with Beatrice to the Mausoleum. After

luncheon saw Janie E., who had just returned, and had
seen the poor Dean. He wished to know my wishes as to
the last sad ceremony. Oh! *what* it means to me to lose
that dear friend who was everything to me from '61 to
the end of '63, being with me at those two dreadful times
in '61! She was such a help in so many ways, so sympa-
thizing, loving, and kind, so attached to me and mine,
so clever and agreeable, known to so many. She used to
write such interesting letters and knew so many interesting
people. It was always a treat to me when she came.'

By the special desire of the Queen, Lady Augusta was
buried in Westminster Abbey, and the eminent position
that she and her husband held in the public life of their
time was shown by the fact that the pall-bearers at the
funeral were the Duke of Westminster, Lord Shaftesbury,
Campbell-Bannerman, Caird, representing the Presbyterian Church of Scotland, Dr. Stoughton, representing Nonconformity, Motley, the historian, representing
America, and Browning, representing literature.

Stanley, a small, delicate, almost over-refined man,
always dependent, never quite recovered from his wife's
death. His friends remained, his relations came to his aid,
his interest in the life about him was not appreciably
lessened, his journeyings continued and included a trip
to the United States, but the years left to him were of
comparatively small distinction. The revision of the New
Testament occupied a considerable part of his time until
1878 when the work was finished. He was still a regular
attendant at the meetings of Convocation and a constant
correspondent to *The Times* and a contributor to the
Edinburgh Review, and perhaps in loyalty to his wife he

remained a persistent advocate and admirer of everything which appealed to the heart of Victoria, and particularly the assumption, at Disraeli's suggestion, of the title Empress of India. Despite the two visits to Russia, he never shared Gladstone's Russophilism. He regarded the Balkan atrocities as exaggerated and was among those many Englishmen who, bitten by one of the most virulent crazes which ever affected the country, professed admiration for the Turk. The Liberal victory in the 1880 election astonished and depressed him, and he grew more and more weary and gloomy. His last work was a volume of essays on Christian Institutions.

He was taken ill suddenly on July 9, 1881, and after receiving the Blessed Sacrament from Canon Farrar, died on July 18. The pall-bearers at his funeral were even more distinguished and 'more comprehensive' than they had been at the funeral of his wife. They were the Duke of Westminster, Temple, then Bishop of Exeter, the President of the Royal Society, Matthew Arnold, Jowett, representing Oxford, and Canon Westcott, representing Cambridge. Stoughton again represented the Nonconformists, for whom Stanley had so warm a place in his heart, Dr. Storey represented the Church of Scotland, and W. H. Smith and W. E. Forster the two parties in the House of Commons. 'No clergyman, perhaps, who ever lived,' said Tait, 'exercised over the public at large, and especially over the literary and thoughtful portion of it, so fascinating an influence as Stanley.'

Stanley was a humanist. He cared, as Colet had cared, for the poor and the unfortunate. He was a man of letters of the order that is rated much more highly by his contemporaries than by succeeding generations. He was a man eager for good works. He was a man of faith, if of a curiously uncoloured and indefinite faith. In all his writings there is, aş his admiring biographer has said, 'a shrinking from theological affirmations, the reticence on questions of doctrine, the reluctance to formulate dogmas.' He desired that the Church of England, which he loved, should be entirely comprehensive, and he realized that it could not permanently be comprehensive unless it arrived at the miraculous state of being an un-dogmatic Church. For half a century the Stanley dream has been made impossible by the development of Anglo-Catholicism with its enthusiastic and vehement repetition of dogmatic belief, and its equally enthusiastic desire again to restore the English Church to union with the great Church of the West. But Stanleyism has reasserted itself, and the production of the Composite Prayer Book may well be the beginning of another chapter in the history of the Church of England, which will make it as inoffensive, as colourless and as comprehensive as Stanley desired.

The Very Rev. William Ralph Inge, D.D., was appointed Dean of St. Paul's by Mr. Asquith in 1911. Like Stanley, he belongs to the clerical aristocracy. His father, also a Doctor of Divinity, was Provost of Worcester College, Oxford, and his maternal grandfather was an Archdeacon. When he married at the mature age of forty-five, he chose as his wife a lady who was the daughter of an Archdeacon and the granddaughter of a bishop. He was educated at Eton and King's College, Cambridge, and after a brilliant university career, he went back to Eton in 1884 as an assistant master. He was tutor of Hertford College, Oxford, from 1889 to 1904, and the vicar of the highly respectable church of All Saints, Ennismore Gardens, from 1905 to 1907. He was Bampton Lecturer in 1889; Lady Margaret Professor of Divinity at Cambridge from 1907 to 1911; Gifford Lecturer in 1917 and Romanes and Hibbert Lecturer in 1920. When Mr. Asquith chose him as successor to Dean Gregory he was known among scholars as a man of profound learning and original thought. But he was almost entirely ignorant of the work of the Church in its connection with the workaday world, and he knew nothing of the doubts and fears, the hopes and aspirations of the average man for whom the Church was created.

Gregory, who was ninety-two when he died in the St. Paul's Deanery, was a child of the Oxford Movement. He had heard Newman preach his last sermon at Littlemore. He was ordained curate to Keble, having Isaac Williams as a colleague. He became Canon of St. Paul's in 1868, and succeeded to the Deanery in 1890. When the Privy Council declared in 1871 that it was illegal to wear Mass vestments and to take the eastward position, Liddon and Gregory ignored the judgment and continued the Catholic practice, and with Church and Liddon, Gregory was responsible for the reform in the Cathedral services which began in the 'seventies with the institution of a Choral Eucharist on Sundays and Holy days.

Gregory had an all-pervading love for his cathedral and for the dignity and beauty of its services. His appearance was impressive. It has been said that 'his face now pale and set in a wealth of long white hair seemed to set the whole tone to the cathedral services and teach all present to pray.' Gregory, who was appointed Dean by the Marquis of Salisbury, succeeded a much greater man. Church who, against his will, accepted the deanery at the suggestion of Gladstone in 1871, first became associated with Anglo-Catholicism when he was elected Fellow of Oriel in 1838, and he was one of the Proctors who saved Newman from official condemnation in 1845. Before coming to St. Paul's he had spent some years in a West-Country living. He and Liddon together made St. Paul's the centre of English religious life. He has been described by Canon Ollard as 'a brilliant writer, a deep thinker and a great preacher, and most of all a man of enormous spiritual power.' As a man of letters he compares almost with Newman himself. As a preacher he was hardly overshadowed by Liddon. Church 1871, Gregory 1890, Inge 1911, that is the story of St. Paul's Cathedral during the last fifty years, and it is a story not without a moral.

It cannot be said that Gregory had the intellectual distinction of either his predecessor or his successor, but

Church, anticipating Dr. Inge, was a man of letters, a scholar and a Bampton Lecturer. The two men are in striking contrast. They represent the two tendencies that have for nearly a century struggled for dominance within the English Church, and they are as different in character as in opinion. The historian of the Oxford Movement declares that 'the lives of the Tractarian leaders were marked by a beauty, a genius, a depth of spiritual power which are a reflection of the life of God,' and of none can this be said more truly than of Church. On the other hand, it is by intellect – cold, hard, detached – that Dean Inge is distinguished. Bernard Shaw once declared with friendly inaccuracy that the Dean is the greatest intellectual asset of the English Church, and even recognizing that this is an exaggeration, it is still true to say that in him there is not only the victory of mind over body, but also, to some extent, the victory of mind over soul.

As it happened, I saw Dr. Inge within a few days on two separate and vastly different occasions. On February 7, 1927, a date which will remain of some importance in the history of the Church of England, when with due solemnity the first draft of the Bishops' proposals for Prayer Book Revision were handed to the members of the two Convocations, Dean Inge sat, as was his right, in a foremost place among the members of the Lower House of Canterbury, between the youthful, eager and almost bustling Dean of Canterbury and the Dean of Westminster, whose appearance suggests the amiability of the minor artist. On the dais were the two Archbishops – His Grace of Canterbury, shrewd, masterful, clear of speech and thought, as he always seems to me, the very type of a Renaissance ecclesiastical statesman; His Grace of York, suaver, less direct, a man of peace. Grouped right and left were the diocesans, wearing the ugly unimpressive Convocation robes, which suggest so little of the proper dignity of princes of the Church.

Dr. Inge had his usual half wistful, half contemptuous expression. He is deaf and presumably did not hear the Archbishop's speech very distinctly. But if he heard he was most assuredly bored. I have never, indeed, seen the Dean at any ecclesiastical function in which boredom was not written all over him, and it is a mystery, which I note without attempting to solve, why a man of his great talent, who holds so little of what is commonly regarded as the Christian faith, should have bothered to have been a Minister of the Church, particularly in these days when, as the Dean's friend, Dr. Hensley Henson, has sorrowfully noted, Holy Orders do not ensure social prestige. Perhaps he is the victim of academic custom and a clerical ancestry.

The second occasion on which I saw Dr. Inge was at the Mansion House at the dinner of a City Company. To me it was an occasion of unqualified dullness. There was much too much to eat and the speeches were prolix and foolish, but Dr. Inge looked considerably more amiable than he did in the Church House. He is, indeed, immensely popular with the City magnates, and is gaining a reputation as a diner-out almost equal to that of the late Archdeacon Sinclair. He, of course, made a speech. It was very short and, in contrast to those that had preceded it, humorous, well phrased and relevant. But it seemed a little sad that the author of *Christian Mysticism* should be obviously happily at home in the company of well-fed

Common Councillors, particularly in view of his often expressed contempt for the protests of the under-fed.

Dr. Inge looks far younger than his sixty-eight years. He has hardly a grey hair. His thin, white face is the typical face of a scholar, marred by an expression that speaks of disillusionment and of scorn. It was once said with a measure of wit that the late Dr. Rashdall, the Modernist Dean of Carlisle, was not a Christian and was sorry, and that Dean Inge was a Christian and was sorry too. In so far as he is a Christian his Christianity is a brand of his own. He is one of the most distinguished of the small eclectic body who call themselves Modern Churchmen and who hold annual conferences in one of the University towns which are attended mainly by highly intellectual-looking young women. But even in this small and select circle Dr. Inge retains his characteristic loneliness. On questions of religion he is largely in agreement with Dr. Barnes, although he has hitherto avoided the Bishop of Birmingham's vulgarities regarding the Holy Eucharist. But Dr. Barnes has sympathies with Labour and was the nominee of a Socialist Prime Minister, and for Labour and Socialism Dr. Inge has nothing but aversion. With Dr. Henson again he has certain affinity and agreement, but there is a curious and unexpected humanity in the Bishop of Durham, whose bark is consistently worse than his bite, which must appear to his friend extremely reprehensible. The Dean will on occasion preach to Nonconformists, but he will not flatter them. The modern Nonconformist is never so happy as when he can secure the patronage of some Latitudinarian or Modernist English ecclesiastic, and they have welcomed Dr. Inge none the less because he has described the Nonconformist conscience with his usual uncomfortable candour.

If the Dean has inherited anything of the love for the Cathedral that characterized Gregory and Church, he manages most successfully to conceal it. Long before it was necessary to shut off a large part of the Cathedral for the work of preservation, it had ceased to have its former immense spiritual significance in the life of the City. With most of the men of his school, the Dean professes a complete contempt for 'ecclesiastical millinery,' and he openly dislikes putting on the cope which Deans are compelled to wear on rare ceremonial occasions. But ceremony is essential to the worship of a cathedral, and however much or little the fact is to be attributed to the Dean's Puritanism, it is certainly true that the glory of St. Paul's has for the time departed – the glory of the days of the influence of Church, the preaching of Liddon, the fostering care of Gregory, the saintly enthusiasm of Scott Holland.

When Dr. Inge went to St. Paul's he was unknown to that larger world which does not habitually read Bampton Lectures and is comparatively unacquainted with Neoplatonic philosophy. But in a very short time he became a newspaper personality. The modern newspaper is uninterested in the normal. The greengrocer who is just a greengrocer, content peacefully to sell his cabbages and potatoes, is never likely to be mentioned in the public press; nor is the Dean who remains just a Dean, preaching in his cathedral and concerned with nothing but his ecclesiastical duties. But the greengrocer who in a fit of wild eccentricity paints his cabbages red, or in a burst of passion murders his placid wife, at once becomes the hero of the headlines. His shop is surrounded by reporters and photographers, and his picture at various periods of his life is printed in the illustrated papers. And similarly with a Dean. He becomes of what is called 'news value' when he develops heterodoxy or eccentricity. Dr. Inge had not long been settled in the Deanery of St. Paul's before in various public utterances he denounced the present and foretold doom in the immediate future. He was at once christened 'the gloomy Dean' by the *Daily Mail*, and he obtained a newspaper notoriety which he has been shrewd enough fully to exploit. The pious dean, the learned dean, even the eloquent dean might have remained unregarded outside ecclesiastical circles, but a gloomy dean was certain of nation-wide fame.

The remote and distant scholar has now become one of the most popular of journalists, and at least two, and sometimes three, articles a week from his pen appear in one newspaper or the other. Generally they are admirable after their own kind, but recently it would seem that Dr. Inge has been rather over-using his journalistic talent, and his writing now tends to be thin and to be the mere repetition of what he has said much better before. It is, however, an important revelation of the character of a very bewildering man that, with his often-repeated scorn of all that is popular, he has not only not disdained to write for the popular press, but that he has set himself to write 'good copy,' articles, that is, for which the sub-editor can find attractive headlines and which even he who runs may read with understanding.

It is the habit of many successful journalists to make picturesque assertions that are quite incapable of proof, and the Dean has shown something like enthusiasm in adopting this custom of his new profession. To quote one example among many, he asserts in his *England* that the Norman Conquest was 'probably a most unmitigated misfortune to England.' The statement is the antithesis of the truth. It is hard to understand how it could have been written by any man of historical knowledge, and it is still more difficult to understand how it could have been written by a Churchman who must necessarily know something of the heavy debt that the English Church owes to the Norman Archbishops – to Lanfranc, to St. Anselm, to Theobald, to St. Thomas.

The Dean is equally fantastic when he writes of his own times. Discussing the question as to whether or not Great Britain could have remained neutral when Germany declared war on France, he suggests that such neutrality must have been followed by an alliance of France with Germany for partitioning the British Empire. English statesmen, he would have us believe, knew if they did not fight with France against Germany, they would have to fight alone against the whole Continent, and they chose the lesser evil. It is possible, of course, that a continental alliance against Great Britain might have occurred after the war with Germany and France had been fought to a finish, but it is sheer nonsense – indeed really bad journalism – to suggest that it was a possibility in August, 1914.

Apart from the workers whom he habitually traduces, and their leaders whom he cannot abide, the Dean has two pet aversions – the Irish and the Roman Catholic Church. He says – I am again quoting from *England*: 'An Englishman is simply unable to comprehend the brooding hatred of the Irishman, who has no better ground than that Cromwell exercised the laws of war somewhat severely against the Irish rebels and that William III won the battle of the Boyne.' Happily, this is simply not true. Many Englishmen – perhaps the majority – find it all too easy to understand the Irish 'brooding hatred.' Few Englishmen, indeed, can recall the history of Ireland during the past three hundred years without a sense of shame, and the shame was not lessened by the exploits of the Black-and-Tans immediately before Great Britain agreed to Ireland's political independence. Dr. Inge is as scornful of the Treaty as he is of the reasons for Irish discontent. Irish loyalists, he says, have been sacrificed 'partly in order to get rid of the nuisance but mainly as part of a determined policy of conciliation towards the United States.' In making such wild suggestions the Dean does not appear to realize how gross are the offences that he gaily attributes to contemporary statesmen and politicians. If he is to be believed, the men responsible for the granting of the Irish Constitution never gave a thought to the demands of justice or to the policy of self-determination to which the whole world paid lip homage at the Paris Conference. To them Ireland was just a nuisance and a bore, and no price was too high to pay for a little peace and quiet. On the other hand, the friendship of the United States was so important that these English statesmen were willing to buy it with the lives and properties of the Irish minority. It is really very dreadful that a Dean of St. Paul's should believe all this – if he really does believe it.

The Dean has no illusions about the United States. I have contended for years that immense mischief has been done by sentimental talk about the blood relation of England and the American Republic, of their common language, common literature, and so on. Nowadays there is certainly no such blood relationship, and it is hardly true to say that there is a common language. Evil must result from the pretence that two peoples fundamentally different in their spiritual qualities and their culture must of necessity share the same ambitions and must always be able to act together. Dr. Inge's references to the United States, therefore, seem to me the most admirable common sense. Mr. Gardiner has said of Dean Inge that 'before you have time to be angry with him for his savage assaults on your pet enthusiasms you have forgiven him for some swashing blow that he has struck at your pet aversion.' It is maddening to me to read his references to Ireland, it is equally refreshing to be reminded that the American Government seriously contemplated taking action against the Allies at the beginning of the Great War, that the American people were sentimentally much more attracted by France than by Great Britain, and that if Great Britain is ever attacked by a European Power 'we may take it as probable that the United States will leave us to our fate.'

When he writes of the Roman Catholic Church the Dean is absolutely reckless in suggestion and assertion. He suggests that the English ideal – self-reverence, self-knowledge, self-control, self-sacrifice – is not in accord with Roman Catholic ethics. He quotes with approval Professor Santayana's assertion that an Englishman – the real, genuine Englishman of course – can never be a Catholic, and he makes the amazing statement that 'it is impossible to converse long with a Catholic without being conscious of an unsurmountable barrier; and if we consider what that barrier is, we find that we cannot confidently appeal to those instincts and moral traditions which are the common heritage of all English people.' Here, of course, the Dean may be quite honestly expressing what has been his own experience when he has gossiped with Cardinal Bourne, Sir Edward Elgar or Mr. Hilaire Belloc, or with any of those Anglo- (to him imitation) Catholics among his fellow-clergy whom he may sometimes meet in the vestry at St. Paul's. But it is an experience which must be so individual as to suggest certain deficiencies in the Dean rather than in his Catholic acquaintance.

With this bold condemnation of Roman Catholics generally, the Dean proceeds to precise statement. In referring to the scandal of 1921, when by a treaty with the Turks for which France was mainly responsible, the Greeks in Asia Minor were left helpless before their enemies and Christianity was practically destroyed with fire and massacre in the home of the Seven Churches, he writes: 'This blow at the Christian religion followed, as I hear on private but good information, an abortive attempt by the Vatican to persuade the Ecumenical Patriarch Meletios to make his submission to the Roman See.' The suggestion apparently is that if Meletios had submitted to Rome – it is certain, of course, that he could have carried only a very small number of the Orthodox with him – the Vatican would have prevented the massacres in Asia Minor, and that, as the Patriarch refused submission, the Vatican permitted the massacres which she could have prevented. The charge is entirely partisan. Certainly the Pope had no such power as the Dean suggests he had, and certainly no reasonable person doubts that he would have used the power if he had possessed it to whatever communion the Christians in Asia Minor belonged, or even if they had been Moslems or Buddhists and not Christians at all.

In one chapter of *England*, after repeating pleasant conventional generalizations, most of them unreliable, about the English character, the Dean goes on to suggest that the workmen of the English cities, from whom he draws away with dislike, are not true blue English. The discipline of Trade Unions and the readiness of the rank and file to obey the orders of their leaders appear to him more un-English than 'the rather superficial Catholic revival.' So far as I know, the Dean has never advocated the teaching of birth prevention methods, but he is convinced that somehow or other the numbers of the rebellious and the unfit must be kept down. It does not seem to occur to him that the destruction of slum areas and the provision of decent conditions of life are the sure and Christian method of making the unfit fit, and the rebellious content. It is demonstrably untrue that a double dose of original sin and abnormal incapacity combine to create the misery and the revolt of the sordid byways of modern cities.

The Dean can discover no satisfactory reason for the prevailing discontent. He says: —

'It is not easy to determine accurately the causes of social unrest. One thing, however, is certain — it is not caused by bad material conditions. There never has been a time in history when comforts and opportunities for recreation were so widely diffused as they are now. The notion that revolutions are caused by misery receives no countenance from impartial history; misery is invented by partial historians to account for the revolution. Discontent is chiefly the result of obscure psychical causes, like unhappiness in the individual. The remedy, if there is a remedy, must be some kind of mind-cure or conversion.

'Partly, however, what we call unrest is aroused simply by the sight of weakly protected wealth. Bee-keepers know that if a mass of honeycomb is left near two hives, the two cities of bees will fight for it till the ground is covered with their corpses. A million years of Communism have not mitigated in the slightest degree the acquisitive instincts of these admirably disciplined insects. If even the bees so far forget themselves, we cannot expect much self-restraint from human beings.'

The one way, apparently, by which contentment may be assured is to make it clear to the 'have nots' that they must remain 'have nots' and must make the best of that condition of life to which it has pleased God to call them. The Dean can find plausible excuse for the assertion that never were 'comforts and opportunities for recreation so widely diffused as they are now.' But he ignores those factors of industrial life that excite anxiety and make for resentment – the constant fear of unemployment, the overcrowded tenements, the hideous mining village, often the insufficient wage. These are the things that revolutions make for: if it is inaccurate to say that misery has never alone caused revolution, in his study of the economic circumstances of the French Revolution, Prince Krapotkin certainly suggests that misery is one of the factors that make revolution inevitable.

The Dean's conception of society is essentially aristocratic. It is for the gifted and cultured few to command

and for the mass to obey. With Nietzsche and Gobineau, the Dean fears that our civilization will come to its end, as the civilizations that have preceded it have come to their end, if the gifted and cultured lose their grip, if, while retaining the desire to command, they have no longer the power to enforce obedience to their orders. The Dean, again with Nietzsche and Gobineau, believes that an aristocracy is doomed when it begins to pity, but unlike both Nietzsche and Gobineau, he will not realize that pity is the very basis of Christianity, and that therefore from the Nietzschean point of view a Christian society cannot exist for very long. Indeed he talks of 'the mawkish travesty of Christianity which transforms morality by basing it on pity.' But unfortunately for the Dean as a minister of the Christian Church, Nietzsche and Gobineau were perfectly right in insisting that this is not 'a mawkish Christianity' but the Christianity that was taught by Our Lord. Pity is the outstanding quality of the Christ, and Dr. Oscar Levy, the most ruthless of Nietzscheans, sneers, and perfectly justifiably as a Nietzschean, at 'the Christianity that wishes to save every soul because it thinks every one perfectible and possibly, if converted to the eternal truth, equal to every one else.' The suggestion of a possible equality is offensive to the aristocratic view, far more offensive than the idea of liberty or of fraternity, and Rousseau, with his teaching of natural rights and his insistence on human equality, moves Dr. Inge to unphilosophic rage. 'The poisonous legacy of Rousseau,' is one of his most characteristic phrases.

In justice it should be remembered that this is an uncomfortable age for the man who really believes that aristocracy is the only possible social rule if civilization and culture are to continue, because it is perfectly evident that human society has embarked on an adventure of democracy which, however it may end, must continue at least for some generations. It cannot be denied that Democracy means in practice mob rule, or rather rule by a minority of astute and unscrupulous persons who have learned how to inflame and direct the mob for their own ends. Nor can it be denied that in the modern world, whenever an experiment is being made in a new form of government which shall at least ensure order, discipline and intelligent and coherent progress, democracy, as it is understood in Great Britain, has first been destroyed. Bolshevism and Fascism are both anti-democratic. Dr. Inge is among the fiercest critics of Bolshevism, first because it is anti-religious, and secondly because in its theory it is designed for the benefit of the mass of the people. And so far as my reading of his voluminous writings has gone, I have not found that he has yet been moved to reasoned defence of Fascism. But he must, if he be consistent, note with approval that both in Russia and Italy there is a minority tyranny, in both cases intelligent, in both cases ruthless, in both cases deliberately ruling the people for the people's good without consulting the people or caring in the least whether the people approve or not. To the Dean the majority must always be wrong, and bitterly as he assails the Catholic Church and the general influence of Catholic priests, his ideal government is obviously a theocracy. I feel that if he really spoke his mind, he would prescribe for the world a government by highly intelligent cardinals, none of whom would really believe the Creeds which it was his duty to repeat.

The fact that the Dean regards democracy as fatal for human society causes him to indulge in diatribes against what has become – to alter Ibsen's famous line – 'the damned compact Labour majority.' As Mr. Gardiner says, President Wilson's dream of making the world safe for Democracy seemed to him 'like talking about making the world safe for smallpox or delirium tremens.' The working man is to the Dean a mere desperado whose one idea is to transfer 'the wealth of the minority to his own pocket.' The worker's political ambition, he says, is to 'levy blackmail on the community under threats of civil war.' He has no morals, no character, no decency. When the Dean thinks of his less lucky fellows who live within a few miles of his comfortable deanery, he has no thought for the hundreds of working men who sacrifice everything for their families, and the thousands of working women who never have a selfish thought. The image that comes to his mind is that of the 'lazy miner who extorts his thousands a year from the households of England, and the bricklayer who battens on the rates and who does about two and a half hours of honest work in a day.' So frenzied is the revolt of his aristocratic soul against the changing conditions of his time that he repeats the banalities natural to the most stupid and prejudiced of die-hard Tories, and is ready to join in the chorus of Conservative ditties sung to the banjo accompaniment of Mr. Rudyard Kipling. In all his many essays on social conditions, there is not the smallest indication that he realizes, what is to most persons of average intelligence an all too obvious fact, that an era in the world's history came to an end in 1914 and that we are standing at the beginning of great social changes which may be brought about with a minimum of destruction and suffering, given good will among the more fortunate, but which will assuredly come about even if the payment has to be made in blood and tears. All that the Dean sees in the modern world is a senseless revolt of the unfortunate against the conditions of their lives, a revolt which common sense demands should be ruthlessly suppressed. He is deaf to the cry for a greater measure of happiness and comfort. He is affronted by the demand to rule on the part of those who have not the capacity to rule, and of the demand of the least worthy to share the good things of the more worthy. And he does not for one moment believe that the Christ, who spent His life among the unworthy and chose to dine with publicans and sinners, must have declared that these demands are entirely justifiable.

Dr. Inge looks out of his deanery windows and sees the world as a steep slope reaching down into the sea. The upper and professional classes are being destroyed by taxation, though he declares that it is a fact beyond argument that 'the children of the upper middle classes are intrinsically far better endowed than the children of unskilled labourers.' The gifted stocks are dying out and power is coming more and more into the hands of 'Trade Union officials and political agitators.' The fact that the classes which the Dean regards as desirable are no longer fecund has compelled him, as I have said, to a half-hearted advocacy of birth prevention. If only the working-class and particularly the more intelligent working-class can be taught to follow their betters along the road of race suicide, then a really proletarian democracy will become more unlikely. The reason for the Dean's backing of the birth-prevention crusade – I repeat that I

realize that it is very qualified — certainly justified the
Roman Catholic lady who, at a recent Labour Congress, denounced the whole business as a device of the
capitalist.

The teetotal fanatic has been properly criticized for the
Manicheanism that finds sin in the wine bottle or the
pint pot rather than in the heart of the drunkard. But
the Dean goes much farther than that. He finds the
explanation for the crime and horror of the slum, not in
the social conditions which bring slums into existence, but
in the evil in the heart of the slum dwellers. Socialists, he
says, are indignant at the suggestion that the pig makes
the sty and not the sty the pig. But that suggestion is
absolutely untrue. Pigs have no natural love for filth, but
it has become a custom to keep them in filthy sties, and
filth and the pig have thus become associated. And the
pretence that the victims of a social system, brought into
being by the industrial revolution and evidently hurrying
towards its uncomfortable end, are selected to suffer
while others benefit because of their lack of moral and
intellectual qualities, falls to the ground with the most
cursory comparison of the less fortunate members of a
modern community with the majority of the more fortunate. Morally, and I believe intellectually, the customers
in a four-ale bar in Stepney are superior to the people
who dance to the tunes of banjos and saxophones till
four o'clock in the morning in the West-End night club,
wasting more money in an evening than the Stepney dock
labourer would spend on his necessities and small
luxuries in a fortnight. The banality of popular plays,
the schoolboy lecherousness of the popular novels, the
ugliness of expensive clothes, all, are the evidence of the

mental and moral decadence of the people who have and who very largely rule because they have. And the Dean realizes this. He knows the particular civilization that he loves is doomed because the aristocrat with traditions and a sense of responsibility has been pushed out by the plutocrat and the political adventurer with no ideals and no scruples. The people who ought to rule no longer possess the necessary courage and ability. But logical as is Dr. Inge's mind, he cannot realize that if it is evident that it is not by virtue alone that the profiteer swells in Berkeley Square, it is evident that it is not by inherent vice alone that the unemployed shrinks to a skeleton in Seven Dials.

But though the comfortable minority is content to be just comfortable, and is indifferent to coming disaster, the Dean remains the complete Nietzschean. The race is for the swift, and it ought to be for the swift. To give the slow even a consolation prize is merely mawkish. The battle is for the strong, and ought to be for the strong, and it is right and proper that the weak should be bashed over the head and should learn to regard the bashing as no more than their deserts. The agitation of the Socialists for a more even distribution of the good things of life, and the misgivings of the sentimental Christians that there is something radically wrong in the arrangement of things as they are, move Dr. Inge to rage. The resentment of the overworked and underpaid against the conditions of their lives, the longing for better houses, greater leisure, more opportunities for enjoying the beauty of the world, all appear to Dr. Inge as merely evidences of spiritual degradation. He says in the second volume of his *Outspoken Essays*: —

'The working-man also has too often no pride and no conscience in his work. He works in the spirit of a slave, grudgingly and bitterly, and then ascribes his unhappiness to the conditions of his employment. He is becoming well educated; but he twists everything round, even religion, to his alleged economic grievances, and loses sight of higher interests. Industrialism drags on, because the alternative is starvation; but the life and joy have gone out of it, and it seems likely to pass into a state of gradual decay. Civilization presents the spectacle of a mighty tree which is dying at the roots. When masses of men begin to ask simultaneously 'Is it all worth while? What is the use of this great Babylon that we have builded?' we are reminded that the mediæval casuists classified *acedia*, which is just this temper, among the seven deadly sins. We had almost forgotten *acedia* and few know the meaning of the word; but it is at the bottom of the diseases from which we are suffering – the frivolous and joyless emptiness of life among the rich, and the bitter discontent of the hand-workers.'

It might occur to another man that it is difficult for the worker to have pride in his work when he has no sort of guarantee that he will have any work next week, and that if he works in the spirit of a slave it is because, to a very large extent, he is a slave. If his life is overshadowed by economic grievances, those grievances must be real and, indeed, they must be utterly damnable if they are sufficiently insistent to cause him to lose all higher interests. It is true that for the great majority of the people, life is characterized as Dr. Inge says 'by a frivolous and joyless emptiness,' but it is difficult to believe that the victims

228

are also the architects of their own undoing. Are they not obviously the victims of a deplorable set of circumstances, the result of vast economic changes which have made interest and joy almost a class monopoly?

Dr. Inge, with all true Nietzscheans, preaches austerity. The superman must be a super-man, not a super-hog. No aristocracy is of any value unless it is an aristocracy of intellect and high ideals. He admits that the short-comings of the capitalist are threatening the existence of the capitalistic system. 'Capitalism is in danger,' he says, 'not so much from the envious attacks of the unpropertied as from the decay of that Puritan asceticism which was its creator.' But some such system as exists to-day must continue if human society is to hold together. Inequality is an unchangeable rule of life. He says: —

'Behind the problem of our own future rises the great question whether any nation which aims at being a work-ing-man's paradise can long flourish. Civilization hitherto has always been based on great inequality. It has been the culture of a limited class which has given its character to the national life, but has not attempted to raise the whole people to the same level. Some civilizations have decayed because the privileged class, obeying a law which seems to be almost invariable, have died out, and the masses have been unable to perpetuate a culture which they never shared.'

Society is dying of softness of the heart. 'Civilization,' Dr. Inge says in *Lay Thoughts*, 'is being poisoned by its own waste products, all the rotten human material that we protect and foster so carefully.' This 'rotten human material' consists of the men and women for whom Our

Lord died, and if the words I have quoted have any real
intention, if the Dean seriously considers that society is
misguided in providing hospitals for the diseased and in
keeping alive the physically imperfect, then he must
obviously favour the lethal chamber for the rotten material
which he resents, and which, judging from the wealth of
his invective, would be extended far beyond those who
are physically maimed to those who in the Dean's view are
mentally and morally twisted, among whom the majority
of the members of the Labour party would most certainly
be counted. 'A painless death for agitators' seems a queer
thing for a Dean to preach, but Dr. Inge is a queer
Dean.

The spacious days of Victoria are for the Dean the
halcyon era of the modern world. There was 'no damned
nonsense' about the Victorians, and, I say it with respect,
there is no damned nonsense about Dean Inge. He would
have spent pleasant evenings with Lord Palmerston and
would probably have not been over-shocked by the exple-
tives of Lord Melbourne. He says quite seriously that
'the grandest and most fully representative figure in all
Victorian literature is Alfred Tennyson,' and in another
place he describes the modern depreciation of Tennyson
as perfectly natural in a generation which will not buy a
novel unless it contains some scabrous story of adultery
and revels in the realism of the man with a muck rake.
To suppose that it is possible not to count Tennyson
among the gods only if one has an over-weening love for
the nasty, is to display an extraordinary limitation both
of critical understanding and of the realization of the
qualities of our age.

The Victorian age excites the Dean's admiration

because it was orderly, prosperous, and, despite the House of Commons, aristocratic, at least until the 'eighties. There was little disturbing unrest. Even when a Victorian lady novelist lived with a man to whom she was not married, she remained a teacher of a Puritanic morality, and one of the less orthodox of the Victorian poets declared that all is well with the world since God is in His Heaven. But Queen Victoria is as dead as Queen Anne. We are living in the age of unrest, and it is clear that the docile society, for which the Dean yearns, can only be possible with the appearance of some individual of phenomenal courage, enterprise and want of heart. The Nietzschean aristocratic society demands the dominating will of a blonde beast. I can see no one who can play the blonde beast in modern England. It is a difficult part for which neither Lord Birkenhead nor Mr. Winston Churchill nor Mr. J. H. Thomas has all the necessary qualities. So it is obvious that the only hope for the world is the appearance some time or the other of a democracy that is intelligent, of a crowd that will not necessarily behave like a mob, of a people that will not be blown hither and thither by every wind of doctrine. Dr. Inge is as certain as M. Gustave le Bon or any other hater of democracy that such an evolution is unthinkable. With his very modern mind and with his over-refined and very openly expressed dislike of the under-refined, he rather oddly shares the mediævalism of Mr. Chesterton. With all his conviction of the essential wrongness of the poor, he is compelled to recognize that they are the victims of social conditions for which humanity is not properly equipped. He says in his *Outspoken Essays:* –

231

'Social unrest is a disease of town-life. Wherever the conditions which create the great modern city exist, we find revolutionary agitation. It has spread to Barcelona, to Buenos Ayres, and to Osaka, in the wake of the factory. The inhabitants of the large town do not envy the country-man ·and would not change with him. But, unknown to themselves, they are leading an unnatural life, cut off from the kindly and wholesome influences of nature, surrounded by vulgarity and ugliness, with no traditions, no loyalties, no culture, and no religion. We seldom reflect on the strangeness of the fact that the modern working-man has few or no superstitions. At other times the masses have evolved for themselves some picturesque nature-religion, some pious ancestor-worship, some cult of saints or heroes, some stories of fairies, ghosts, or demons, and a mass of quaint superstitions, genial or frightening. The modern town-dweller has no God and no Devil; he lives without awe, without admiration, without fear. Whatever we may think about these beliefs, it is not natural for men and women to be without them. The life of the town artisan who works in a factory is a life to which the human organism has not adapted itself; it is an unwholesome and unnatural condition. Hence, probably comes the *malaise* which makes him think that any radical change must be for the better.

'Whatever the cause of the disease may be (and I do not pretend that the conditions of urban life are an adequate explanation) the malady is there, and will probably prove fatal to our civilization.'

The crowded streets of a city produce revolution because the crowded streets of a city are not suited to the nature of man. I do not think that the Dean has considered the very interesting question as to whether, even with the elaboration of the machinery of production, the city must necessarily continue. Suppose that power were created at great centres and distributed, as it may well be one of these days, by wireless, is it not possible that production would be as economic and efficient in village workshops as it is now in the more or less unwholesome factories of smoke-begrimed cities? The suggestion of the passage that I have quoted is that it is bad for men to be cooped up too closely together, that a wholesome life demands space and a measure of privacy, and space and privacy are the two things that the city worker is entirely denied.

The criticism of the Dean as a social thinker is that he has no considered policy to advocate because he has so little sympathy to offer. He is a physician who can diagnose but cannot prescribe. He realizes that society is in a bad way. He has a shrewd idea of the nature of the disease. But when he comes to discuss remedies, he retreats into an almost sentimental vagueness which is alien to his temperament. In dealing with the workaday world he is only effective in invective. It is characteristic of him, too, that, loud as is his denunciation and bitter as is his scorn for the Socialist and the Labour agitator, he would be almost equally as uncomfortable as a member of the anti-Socialist Union as he would be as a member of the Independent Labour party. He is not to be deceived by shibboleths and he is constitutionally antagonized by slogans. If Commander Locker-Lampson could be persuaded to stand outside the deanery windows for eight hours a day shouting at the top of his voice 'All Socialists are in the pay of Moscow,' before the end of the week Dean Inge would assuredly become a member of the Labour Party.

Somewhere or the other he speaks appreciatively of the patriotism of Henley and Kipling, but his own patriotism is much less theatrical. He showed a notable restraint and Christian sanity during the war, and in a sermon soon after the Armistice he declared: 'We cannot afford to have a humiliated embittered degenerate Germany any more than a triumphant militant Germany.' He is a patriot, but in a fine way. 'This much I can avow,' he says, 'that never even when storm clouds appear blackest have I been tempted to wish that I were other than an Englishman.' Mr. Gardiner has well said: 'He is as scornful of Imperialism as he is of Socialism. He is a good European and never talks the cant of patriotism. The greatness of his country is not a material thing and does not depend on painting the map red. It is a moral and spiritual thing that has been our noblest contribution to the world.'

There is no greater illusion about the English than that they are a hard-headed people with a genius for business and commerce. Years ago in the preface to *John Bull's Other Island*, Bernard Shaw perfectly justly gibed at the English as a nation of romantics. The Empire was founded by men who really cared next to nothing for the commercial success of their venture but who journeyed round the earth inspired by the spirit of adventure and that fidgetiness which is a national characteristic. 'J'y suis, j'y reste,' is the motto of the great majority of the French. 'Here we are, for Heaven's sake, let's go somewhere else!' is the motto of the English, and generally it is true to say that the only Englishman who stays at home is the Englishman who has not sufficient money to buy a railway ticket. 'It may be doubted,' says Dr. Inge, 'whether nature intended the Englishman to be a money-making animal.' As a matter of fact, the Englishman very rarely is a money-making animal. The majority of great fortunes made in this country belong to intelligent aliens, either from Ireland or more distant countries. The Englishman has no idea of thrift, and, again as Dr. Inge points out, he has never mastered the art of spending money. He is the romantic and the fact that he often blunders through is the measure of his romanticism. The unpractical often inherit the earth, since they rush in, in complete safety, when the cautious and intelligent angels are afraid to cross the threshold. Few will quarrel with Dean Inge's statement: —

'We believe in chivalry and fair play and kindliness — these things first and foremost; and we believe, if not exactly in democracy, yet in a government under which a man may think and speak the thing he wills. We do not believe in war, and we do not believe in bullying, we do not flatter ourselves that we are the supermen; but we are convinced that the ideas which we stand for, and which we have on the whole tried to carry out, are essential to the peaceful progress and happiness of humanity.'

But with all the fine qualities of the English, which he ungrudgingly admits, the Dean is inclined to believe that England has passed its zenith. Maybe, he says, as it were with a scornful shake of the head, 'our mission as a world power is nearly accomplished. If that is so, there is a goodly record to the nation's credit and she may look forward to a comfortable and not unhappy future in grandmotherly satisfaction at the achievement and character of her descendants.

Dr. Inge has frequently been compared with his great predecessor, Donne. In his interesting book *In Defence of the Faith*, Mr. Charles Gardner says: 'The two men have much in common — wide and deep learning, a restless and inquisitive intellect, a melancholy complexion, a satiric pen and a polished disdain.' This is admirable rhetoric, but it is very little more. Donne was an artist. Dr. Inge is a philosopher. Donne's attitude to life was the result of uncomfortable circumstances and considerable disappointment. Dr. Inge would seem to have found most of the things that he sought if not most of the things that he wanted, and the disdain that Mr. Gardner finds in Dr. Inge is much more kin to that of Swift than to that of Donne. The late H. W. Massingham said of Swift: 'He hated human passion, having indeed a fearfully sharpened sense of the part it played in his own life and in the world of war and politics and sensual intrigue into which he was born.' One of Dr. Inge's outstanding characteristics is a similar hatred of sensualism in every form. He is definitely and thoroughly a Puritan, and in this he resembles both Swift and Bernard Shaw. In his acute character study of the Dean, Mr. A. G. Gardiner emphasizes the resemblance between Dr. Inge and Mr. Shaw. 'His' (Dr. Inge's) 'genius for controversy is only matched by that of Mr. Bernard Shaw, with whom he has much in common in spite of the wide disparity in their views and professions. Mr. Shaw is, of course, much nearer the accepted Christian ethic. He lashes us but he loves us, tolerates, in a way believes in us. He has pity and compassion, in a word he is humanitarian.' As Mr. Gardiner points out, no one fills Dr. Inge with quite so much rage as a humanitarian. He lashes us, too, but he certainly does not love us. In his whole-hearted defence of Swift, Mr. Charles Whibley says: 'He loved such of his friends as he deemed worthy of his love with an unchanging loyalty, but did not close his eyes to the general infamy of mankind. . . . Since he did not waste his affection upon the vague thing called humanity, he had all the more to spare for those friends who loved and understood him.' It is certainly true to say that so far as one can judge from his public statement, Dr. Inge also does not waste his affection on 'that vague thing called humanity.' He has for the crowd a contempt equal to that of Nietzsche and of Ibsen in his bitterest moods.

Dr. Inge's first published work was his Bampton Lectures, *Christian Mysticism*, published in 1899. The ever-increasing interest in mysticism in our time is part of the reaction against Victorian materialism, and it is not without a suggestion of irony that a writer to whom the Victorian era is the golden age should have done much to stimulate the Georgian understanding of the mystics. The mystic contrives to live in close and intimate personal communion with God Who is to him supreme and all attractive. To the mystic it has been finely said God ceases to become an object and becomes an experience. Writing with the fullness of knowledge, Dr. Inge analyses and explains the teaching of the great mystics and the development of mysticism, and always with the underlying suggestion that there is no necessary conflict between the spiritual and the material. Mr. Gardner has remarked the fact that of the most famous mystics, Blake alone is neglected, and he suggests that the Dean's ignoring of

Blake is to be found in the fact that there was in him 'an ocean of sensualism.' There are in *Christian Mysticism* many suggestions of the teaching which Dr. Inge has elaborated in more recent years. He is always and emphatically a Protestant. He writes: —

'We cannot shut our eyes to the fact that both the old seats of authority, the infallible Church and the infallible book, are fiercely assailed, and that our faith needs reinforcements. These can only come from the depths of the religious consciousness itself; and if summoned from thence, they will not be found wanting. The "impregnable rock" is neither an institution nor a book, but a life of experience. Faith, which is an affirmation of the basal personality, is its own evidence and justification. Under normal conditions, it will always be strongest in the healthiest minds. There is and can be no appeal from it. If, then, our hearts, duly prepared for the reception of the Divine Guest, at length say to us, "This I know, that whereas I was blind, now I see," we may in St. John's words, "have confidence towards God." '

This is exactly the point of view of the sixteenth-century reformers. Guidance is to be obtained not from any external authority, but from internal and individual consciousness. Everything, that is to say, is to be judged by experience, and from individual experience there can be no appeal. Here, indeed, is the reiteration of what I have suggested was the basis of Dean Stanley's teaching, 'Let everybody be religious in his own way.' It is always 'our own hearts' to which we are to look for guidance. 'Our hearts tell us,' Dr. Inge says, 'of a higher form of existence in which the doom of death is not merely deferred but abolished.' And he takes no notice of the very apparent fact that the hearts of a large number of people tell them nothing of the sort and that, therefore, if we are to be logical, we are compelled to believe that life continues for those who believe it will continue and abruptly ends for those who believe that the graveyard is the end of the human story. In Christian Mysticism Dr. Inge writes, of course, as one having authority and not as the scribes. There is no uncertainty about his assertions. He does not fear to pontificate. For example he says, 'It has been abundantly proved that neither Romanism nor Protestantism regarded as alternatives possesses enough of the principle to satisfy the religious needs of the present day.' Nothing of the sort has been proved or can be proved. To the Romanist and to the Protestant his individual faith possesses all the truth or it is valueless. This sort of assertion has been common in all the ages from men dissatisfied with established religions and eager to invent a religion of their own.

Dr. Inge tells us that the special work assigned to the Church of England would seem to be the development of a Johannine Christianity which shall be 'both Catholic and Evangelical without being either Roman or Protestant.' I confess that to me this is absolutely meaningless. I cannot conceive of any form of Christianity which might not roughly be called either Roman or Protestant, for it is quite impossible to think of a Catholic Christianity which would not in its essence be Roman, or of a genuine revolt against Romanism which must not be Protestant. But it is the way of the superior reformer to scorn the systems that he inherits, and if in the circumstances it is impossible for him to devise some enticing new and original faith, to imagine an impossible combination that shall have its own peculiar characteristics.

Another of the Dean's prejudices is apparent when in *Christian Mysticism* he refers to 'Teutonic civilization.' There is no such thing. European civilization is Latin civilization, and the very quality which the Dean attributes to Teutonic civilization, its high standard of domestic life, was just that quality of Roman civilization, in the days before the Empire, that differentiated it from the Greek civilization which it succeeded. With this phrase, 'Teutonic civilization,' the true Victorian speaks, and particularly the Victorian divine who having learned from German theologians to doubt the Christian verities persuades himself that every good thing was imported from across the Rhine.

I quote one more passage from *Christian Mysticism:* —

'The fact that human love or sympathy is the guide who conducts us to the heart of life, revealing to us God and Nature and ourselves, is proof that part of our life is bound up with the life of the world, and that if we live in these our true relations we shall not entirely die so long as human beings remain alive upon this earth. The progress of the race, the diminution of sin and misery, the advancing Kingdom of Christ on earth, — these are matters in which we have a *personal* interest. The strong desire that we feel — and the best of us feel it most strongly — that the human race may be better, wiser, and happier in the future than they are now or have been in the past, is neither due to a false association of ideas nor to pure unselfishness. There is a sense in which death would not be the end of everything for us, even though in this life only we had hope in Christ.'

The assertion with which this passage begins is true, but only partially true, and likely to lead to dangerous illusion unless it is very radically qualified. It suggests the immortality of the Comtist, the life of a good man continuing in the regenerative power of his influence even after his death, rather than the doctrine of immortality of the Catholic Church. With the rest of the passage there can be little quarrel, and I only quote it since it is in striking contrast to the pessimism of the Dean's more recent diatribes against his fellows. There is a definite assertion of a belief in progress for the whole of humanity to a higher, nobler and more satisfying life.

The general study of mysticism led Dr. Inge to set himself to the most considerable achievement of his life, *The Philosophy of Plotinus*, which, though it was not published until 1918, was the result of years of study and thought. It was, indeed, preceded by the publication just before the war of a much slighter book, *The Religious Philosophy of Plotinus and some Modern Philosophies of Religion*. 'With the aid of Plotinus,' says Mr. Charles Gardner, 'Dean Inge has found himself and knows his own mind.' And it is not without its significance that the Dean of St. Paul's should be the spiritual child of the great third century non-Christian Neoplatonist, that he should derive from Plotinus and not from Origen.

Plotinus, the philosopher and mystic, conceived the world as dominated by an infinite and omnipresent God from whom all things come while 'all derived existence has a drift towards, a longing for the higher and bends towards it so far as its nature permits.' The soul degraded by its connection with the material body – there is more than a suggestion of Manicheanism in the teachings of Plotinus – can by the practice of virtue and rigid asceticism first return to its best self, and then find its way back to God in an experience of mystical ecstasy. Dean Inge says: –

'According to Plotinus, when we pass from visible and audible beauty to the beauty which the Soul perceives without the help of the senses, we must remember that we can only perceive what is akin to ourselves – there is such a thing as soul-blindness. Incorporeal things are beautiful when they make us love them. But what constitutes their beauty? Negatively, it is the absence of impure admixture. An ugly character is soiled by base passions; it is like a body caked with mud; in order to restore its natural grace it must be scraped and cleansed. This is why it has been said that all the virtues are a purification. The purified soul becomes a form, a meaning, wholly spiritual and incorporeal. The true beauty of the Soul is to be made like to God. The good and beautiful are the same, and the ugly and the bad are the same. The Soul becomes beautiful through Spirit; other things, such as actions and studies, are beautiful through Soul which gives them form. The Soul too gives to bodies all the beauty which they are able to receive.'

In this striking passage there is certainly no contradiction of Catholic doctrine. Plotinus was unaffected by Christian teaching, but he, with Origen, was the heir of the earlier Greek philosophies that vitally affected the development of Christian thought. The beauty of purity, the ugliness of sin are emphasized in the teaching of Our

Lord Himself. 'Blessed are the pure of heart: for they shall see God.' And the possibility of the soul's return to God is to Dr. Inge the possible approximation to the nature and character of Our Lord. He writes: —

'Nor is it quite correct to deny all progress within the historical period. There are, after all, horrors described in the Old Testament, in Greek history, in Roman history, in mediæval history, which only the Bolsheviks have rivalled, and which indicate a degree of depravity which we may perhaps hope that civilized humanity has outgrown. And if there has been perceptible progress in the last two thousand years, the improvement may be considerable in the next ten thousand, a small fraction, probably, of the whole life of the species. The Soul of the race is no demon, but a child with great possibilities. It is capable of what it has already achieved in the noblest human lives, and the character which it has accepted as the perfect realization of the human ideal is the character of Christ.'

To the Plotinian philosophy the Dean adds a profound veneration for the character of Christ, and he emerges, a figure new and strange, the Neoplatonist Christian. In the struggle between Cyril of Alexandria and Hypatia he would have been partly with Cyril and partly with Hypatia, but much more with the philosopher than with the bishop, whom Charles Kingsley has so enthusiastically misrepresented.

The Dean's conception of life as a soul's upward adventure lends to a resentment of the tyranny of the material. 'A restoration of internal and external peace,' says Dr. Inge, 'is possible only when we rise to the vision of the real, the spiritual world.' And he insists that the Christian doctrine of spiritual progress is true: —

'Love and suffering cut the deepest channels in our souls, and reveal the most precious of God's secrets. Even in national life we can see that the characteristic utterances of ages of prosperity — the Augustan Ages of history — are less penetrating and of less universal significance than those which have been wrung from nations in agony.'

The way of salvation is hard, but it lies open for all. But salvation is only to be gained by the united effort of every part of a man's being: —

'Mysticism is a spiritual philosophy which demands the concurrent activity of thought, will, and feeling. It assumes from the outset that these three elements of our personality, which in real life are never sundered from each other, point towards the same goal, and if rightly used will conduct us thither. Further, it holds that only by the consecration of these three faculties in the service of the same quest can a man become effectively what he is potentially, a partaker of the Divine nature and a denizen of the spiritual world. There is no special organ for the reception of Divine or spiritual truth, which is simply the knowledge of the world as it really is. Some are better endowed with spiritual gifts than others, and are called to ascend greater heights; but the power which leads up the pathway to reality and blessedness is, as Plotinus says, one which all possess, though few use it.'

And the Dean has a glimmering hope that humanity as a whole may one day arrive at felicity: —

'The ascent of the soul to God, which is made by thousands in the short span of a single life, may be an earnest of what humanity shall one day achieve.'

But the only possible progress is spiritual. The Dean has no faith in 'a delusive millennium on earth.'

This gospel of the Neoplatonist Christian is useless to the workaday world. The suggestion that every man may work out his salvation if he will is a delusion. It is no use urging the Mrs. Dombeys of this world to make an effort. Our Lord instituted His Church because it was certain that men would be destroyed without a sanctuary, and lost without a guide. For the vast majority, the ascent from the basest to the highest can only be attained by constant supernatural help, by fasting and contemplation maybe, but most certainly by confession, absolution and prayer, and by the grace vouchsafed in the sacraments of Holy Church. What is the message of Plotinus and Dr. Inge to the starving tramp, the disgruntled harlot, the detected swindler or to the harassed mother of a large family, the heart-broken mourner, the man sick of his own meanness and unable to escape from it? Plotinus has no place in a Christian cathedral.

Steeped as he is in the philosophy of Plotinus, it is natural that the Gospel of St. John should appeal to Dean Inge more than the more clear-cut assertions of the synoptic writers. He says in *Truth and Falsehood and Religion*: 'I think the questions as to the manner of the Incarnation and of the Resurrection may safely be left alone by those who are convinced that the Word was made Flesh, and tabernacled among us.' He certainly does not deny the facts of the Virgin Birth and the empty

tomb, but he regards them as of a quite secondary importance. He would probably deny that Our Lord Himself
had ever founded the Catholic Church, and he is insistent
that Christ Himself would have been among those whom
the Church has persecuted. He has written: —

'Christ Himself, if He had returned to earth in the
Middle Ages, would certainly have been burnt alive for
denying the dogmas about His own nature. The hierarchy
would have recognized in Him with more alacrity than
Caiaphas did, the most deadly enemy of all that they
meant by religion. For Christ was primarily concerned
with awakening into activity the consciousness of God in
the individual soul: His parting promise was that this
consciousness should be an abiding possession of those
who followed in His steps. He declared war against the
orthodoxies and hierarchies of His time.

'The path of life, as He showed it by precept and
example, was superior to anything that either Greeks or
Indians traced out, but the conception of salvation is
essentially the same — a growth in the power of spiritual
communion by a consecrated life of renunciation and
discipline. His Kingdom of God was a spiritual fellowship of those who were "baptized with the Holy Ghost." '

Here there is a repetition of the Plotinus doctrine
accepted in part, but only in part, by all Christian philo-
sophers, that salvation comes from renunciation and discipline. But Dr. Inge seems to ignore the importance of
faith and prayer.

The detached position of the Dean is immensely interesting. While he is the antithesis of a materialist, with a
Puritan horror of sensual emotion and an unqualified

acceptance of the teaching that the unseen is of immensely greater importance than the seen, as I understand him, he is unable to believe in the possibility of the occasional and, if I may use the term, eccentric interference with the ordinary course of ordinary affairs. He believes that God is omnipotent and all-pervading, but he is not prepared to affirm that at any time in the history of the human race God has interfered with any of the laws which He Himself has made. The miracles of Our Lord, the Virgin Birth, the Resurrection, the Ascension into Heaven, may be Greek legends welded on to the Gospel story, and Our Lord remains just the figure of a man in perfect accord with beneficent omnipotence who, appearing among a small and fiercely patriotic people earnestly praying for a national revival, told them with 'unpatriotic pessimism' that they should not demand such a narrow millennium, but that they should strive to attain a spiritual and moral emancipation. So they crucified Him, not as the Gospel teaches as an atonement for the sins of humanity and as a direct means of effecting a reconciliation between God and His creatures, but because of the common natural man's instinctive resentment against the teacher of that Neoplatonist scheme of salvation which demands from him the disciplined effort which he abhors.

Supposing that Dean Inge is a safe and reliable guide, and that his view of the mission of Our Lord is to be accepted, then God becomes, not the father of all men, but merely the father of the supermen, and the rest of us are left out in the cold. The doctrine is Calvinism in a more horrid and exclusive sense, for the Calvinist may believe that the simple and the undisciplined and the blundering are possibly among the elect, while

Dr. Inge's Heaven would in practice be reserved for men and women capable of taking a double first. It would be a thinly populated Heaven, and a very dull one. I can conceive no society more tiresome than that of the sanctified prig.

Mr. Charles Gardner has said that 'Dr. Inge holds a place that was temporarily held by Augustine before he became a Christian.' If this be true, the conclusion is that it is a position that no Christian can hold. 'He reads Christ in the light of Neoplatonism instead of Neoplatonism and other things in the light of Christ. He is a genius of philosophy but somehow has missed the genius of Christ's Christianity.' Presumably Dr. Inge repeats the Nicene Creed at least once a week, and if one is to judge him from his published essays, there can hardly be a clause in that Creed which he could repeat without some qualification or without using terms in some entirely arbitrary and personal sense. This, of course, is not unusual in the Church of England, and Dr. Inge is in much the same boat as Dean Stanley and the other nineteenth century Latitudinarians. It is, however, worth pointing out, at a time when the episcopal dignitaries of the Church are threatening prosecution for those of her ministers who believe too much, how very little a high dignitary of the Church can believe without running the smallest risk.

The Neoplatonist Christianity of which Dr. Inge is the most distinguished if not the only professor, may be a religion satisfying to a scornful intellect, but it is not the Christianity of the Gospels, it is not the Christianity of the Creeds, it is not the Christianity of the Catholic Church. Its precepts of self-discipline and the responsibility that each man has for his own destiny are valuable and not to be ignored, but happily for us it is not true that we are the architects of our own fortunes. We are not the sport of the gods, but we are the children of God, dowered with a sufficient measure of free will to hasten or to hinder the day of release, but unable, however capricious we may be, ultimately to escape from the Hound of Heaven. There is a far greater appreciation of the Christian Church in Shakespeare than in the whole of the many volumes of Plotinus: —

> 'There's a divinity that shapes our ends
> Rough-hew them as we will.'

The Dean's aristocratic faith has inspired his aristocratic contempt for those unfortunates, incidentally the vast majority of the human race, who are unable, alone and unaided, to toil up the steep, hard road that leads to perfection.

With all his scorn for Rousseau and the philosophy of the French Revolution, the Dean might well have worshipped at the shrine of the revolution's Goddess of Reason. 'I am the captain of my soul,' exclaimed Henley in a frenzy of self-deception, and in the same spirit the Dean declares: 'I will play no tricks with my soul.' Other people may play-act, but he will have nothing to do with make-believe. He has no sort of idea, to quote a fine sentence of Mr. Chesterton's, that 'fairyland is nothing but the sunny country of common sense.' And with all men who have no conception of the meaning of fairyland, the Dean is fated to spend his life in the seats of the scornful.

The contest in the Church of England between the

Catholics who fervently believe in the doctrine of the objective Real Presence of Our Lord in the Sacrament of the Altar, and the Protestants who regard such belief as degrading idolatry, simply bores the Dean. He is a Protestant in so far as he rejects Catholic teaching, but he has no sympathy with the fanatics of the 'Protestant underworld,' to use Dr. Henson's phrase, who grow wrathful or tearful when Catholic practice is permitted. Like Gallio he cares for none of these things. He dislikes religious earnestness whether it is demonstrated in preaching at the street corner or in celebrating Mass with proper beauty and dignity. He is the clerical first cousin of Gilbert's Mr. Blake: —

'I have known him indulge in profane, ungentlemanly emphatics,
When the Protestant Church has been divided on the subject of the width of a chasuble's hem;
I have even known him to sneer at albs – and as for dalmatics,
Words can't convey an idea of the contempt he expressed for *them*.'

The Dean traces all the phenomena of modern life which he detests, to the same cause, the abandonment of reason, that reason which he declares was given to him that 'I may know things as they are,' a claim which for complete arrogance it would be hard to match. He writes in *Lay Thoughts*: —

'This epidemic of irrationalism has given us pragmatism in philosophy, magic and superstition in religion, antinomianism in morals, post-impressionism in art, and

Bolshevism in politics. At least they all come from the father of lies, so I suppose they are closely related to each other, and I think I can see some relation between them. They all begin by saying: "The true is what I choose to believe, and if I choose persistently enough I can make it so." '

I am bold enough to suggest that this fine-sounding pronouncement is as essentially absurd as it is intentionally offensive. Examine it in detail. Pragmatism in philosophy may be evil, but the doctrine that 'the proof of the pudding is in the eating' can hardly be dismissed as irrational. Antinomianism is I admit utterly damnable, but it is in effect an exaggerated interpretation of the doctrine of justification by faith. By 'magic and superstition in religion' Dr. Inge obviously refers to faith in the objective Presence. That may be denounced as unreasonable or defended as super-reasonable, but it is merely capricious to find affinity of type in the Catholic who accepts the Catholic teaching with all its very trying obligations in the individual life to the antinomianist who believes that, because he is saved, he can riot and wanton without the smallest fear of consequences. Post-impressionism may be the invention of the father of lies, but no more and no less than any other experiment in artistic expression, and I feel quite certain that if the Dean had published his *Lay Thoughts* fifty years earlier, he would have written Pre-Raphaelitism for Post-Impressionism. And to say that Bolshevism is irrational is unadulterated nonsense. The Bolshevist is so supremely dangerous because he is so supremely rational. He is the only politician in the world to-day who has a clear-cut philosophy which he is endeavouring to translate into action, and a politician who is also a philosopher is a much more dangerous person than the ordinary politician who has not only no philosophy but is generally quite incapable of connected thought. To say of a Bolshevist that he begins with the assertion that 'truth is what I choose to believe and if I choose persistently enough I can make it so' is sheer prejudice, unworthy of a thinker of Dean Inge's distinction.

When he is angry, the Dean is quite incapable of reasoned argument. He works himself up into a fit of righteous rage and bashes away at the minxes, caring for nothing except to deal mighty blows and to raise mighty bruises. And having convinced himself that apart from a very thin remnant of the intellectual elect, who have not yet bowed the knee in the temple of the Baal of material success, the rich are vulgar, the poor are degraded, the middle classes have lost the Puritan sense of duty – the Dean sees the whole world going to the 'demnition bow-wows.' But his pessimism is not unqualified. He is not as hopeless as Anatole France. He possesses that glimmer of faith in the future which Thomas Hardy professes in one passage in *The Dynasts*. I quote from *England:* –

'In plain living and high thinking will be our salvation, or the salvation of the "remnant" which will survive the turmoils of an age of transition. Plain living will be forced upon us, whether we will or not, for the conditions of prosperity are in part slipping from us, and in part are being wantonly thrown away; high thinking will not only make us citizens of the City "whose type is laid up in heaven," but will mitigate the acerbities of a struggle for which the responsibility cannot be laid solely on the shoulders of any one class. Aristotle would teach us that "to be always seeking after utilities does not become free and elevated souls," and that "we must train the nobler sort of natures not to desire more than they have got." But the New Testament is equally insistent that whatever work we have to do must be done "heartily, as to the Lord and not to men," and that those who will not work have no claim on the community for maintenance. Still more decisive is the warning that a house divided against itself cannot stand.'

But there is a gentle dean as well as a gloomy and scornful dean. And the gentle dean is startlingly revealed in the touching description, never over-strained, sincere, beautiful in its phrasing, of the death of his little daughter, Margaret Paula, who died in Holy Week, 1923. He writes – and no one can doubt him: –

'It is not congenial to me to tear aside the veil which secludes the sanctities of a happy home.'

And he adds with restrained pride: –

'It has been my strange privilege, as I believe, to be the father of one of God's saints, a character as pure and beautiful as many which are recorded in the Church's Roll of Honour.'

And the chapter in his *Personal Religion*, in which he writes of his daughter, concludes as follows: –

'I hope my readers will not think that I have said too much about our little girl. There are, thank God, countless other beautiful child characters, and many may justly

think that their own children are not less worthy of com-
memoration. But let what I have written be taken as a
reverent tribute to the child nature, which our Saviour
loved and bade us imitate. At a time when so much of our
literature is strangely blind to the glory and excellence of
human nature at its best, I do not think we can be blamed
for making known what we have ourselves seen of the
beauty of holiness in a short life, and for showing, as the
letters which I have quoted and many others like them
have shown, how many sweet natures there are in the
world, swift to recognize and love that beauty when they
see it in another. Some will, I hope, be reminded of children who, like our little daughter, have been lent them for
a time and then taken home into the presence of the Lord
of little children. For we ought to remember them, and
"keep our memory green" for those sad but blessed
experiences of our human lot. Some may perhaps have
the same feeling that we have, that there may be a wonderful completeness in a life which only lasted a few years.
"She, being made perfect in a short time, fulfilled a long
time, for her soul was dear to the Lord." '

So the Dean reveals the man of deep human affection
and firm faith, hidden behind the hard exterior of that
other man angered by the follies of his age and unable to
refrain from sneers and gibes at his weaker brethren. It
is not remarkable that Dr. Inge should have loved his
daughter, that he should have admired her dainty qualities,
that he should have grieved for her early death, but it is
remarkable that he should have told the world of his love
and his grief, that he should have been impelled to admit
the great public, for which he habitually has nothing but

disdain, across the sacred portals of his home at a time
when he might have been expected to have double-barred
the doors. He has written what is for a man of his mind
and temper an almost pathetic request to the world to
share his sorrow and to understand his loss, an invitation
to the wayfarer to drop a violet on the dead child's grave.
I confess when I read the Dean's sneers at the poor, his
attacks on the Labour party, his jeers at Anglo-Catholics
and the Catholic faith, I recall this slight, beautiful story
of Margaret Paula, and in the apparent inconsistencies
I discover humanity in this austere and lonely man of
genius.